Heal Your Brain: Heal Your Body

Esly Regina Carvalho, Ph.D.

TraumaClinic
Edições

Heal Your Brain: Heal Your Body

*How EMDR Therapy Can Heal
Your Body
by Healing Your Brain*

Esly Regina Carvalho, Ph.D.

Heal Your Brain: Heal Your Body
How EMDR Therapy Can Heal Your Body by Healing Your Brain

This book is part of the series
Clinical Strategies in Psychotherapy, Volume 2

Originally published in Portuguese, 2015

ISBN 13: 978-1-941727-31-7
ISBN 10: 1-941727-31-X

Cover art: Claudio Ferreira
Translation: Esly Regina Carvalho, Ph.D.
Layout: Marcella Fialho

TraumaClinic Edições
SEPS 705/905 Ed. Santa Cruz sala 441
70.390-755 Brasília, DF Brasil
+ 55 (61) 3443 8447
www.traumaclinicedicoes.com.br
vendas@traumaclinicedicoes.com.br

Table of Contents

Presentation

Like so many others, this book was also born out of my experiences with my patients, from whom I learn so much. When I was still a fairly new psychotherapist, I saw a young lady who had a congenital heart problem. She needed open-heart surgery, with all of its risks, in order to make the correction. Rose finally decided to face this major intervention because she had really run out of options. She knew that if she didn't go through with the surgery she could literally drop dead at any moment so great was her health risk. We did the preparatory pre-surgery therapy work, said emotional good-byes, and Rose went to a foreign country specialized in that kind of surgery.

A few months later, she booked an appointment. The surgery had been wildly successful, but now Rose was afraid she was going to die! Precisely when she no longer had any physical heart risk…? I was mystified. We spent several months working together until her fear finally receded and resolved. Slowly, I began to put it together. Rose's *body* began to really "believe" in the real and imminent risk of death only *after* the operation. Before the surgery, it was just her logical, linear brain that had understood the importance of going through with it. After the surgery, it was her body that "understood" what could have happened to her. That's when her fear of dying emerged. Her body believed in what her mind had only thought about before.

As a result, I reached a very simple, obvious conclusion: we were created in such a way that stuff on the inside should stay on the inside, and stuff on the outside should stay on the outside. That's what skin is for – to delineate what's in and what's out. The body was not made to be opened up or operated. Is it necessary? Of course! But the *body does not like it*. Surgeries, wounds, lesions, injuries – all have consequences, sometimes much greater than we ever imagined.

The proposal of this book is to demonstrate how EMDR therapy can bring healing and relief to issues related to the body: illnesses, pain, medical procedures, surgeries, difficult diagnoses, and living with chronic disease. I hope these illustrations of how we can use these clinical strategies will bring hope and relief to people in pain. It was written for the general public, so that anyone can read and follow the stories that are shared within its pages. It is our hope that more and more people will come to know the healing power of EMDR therapy. Psychotherapists that have been trained in this approach will easily understand the structure of the sessions. Hopefully, they will be able to implement these suggestions with their clients. Other professionals who still have not been trained can seek out accredited training courses. (Check out the EMDR Institute at www.emdr.com.)

In the case studies in this book, we show how EMDR therapy can be used specifically for illnesses, medical interventions and the resolution of physical symptoms of traumatic origin. Neurobiology has slowly begun to help us understand this. For deeper look at the research on neurobiology and illnesses with an unknown medical origin, see Dr. Uri Bergmann's book, *Neurobiological Foundations for EMDR Practice*.[1]

In this book we also share a study with 17 thousand participants that points to how adverse childhood experiences (ACE) plays a part in the development of serious illnesses in adulthood, and therefore why treating trauma is imperative to healing and even preventing serious disease in adulthood.[2] EMDR therapy is especially useful in unlocking these traumas and allowing healing to flow through the brain neurochemistry.

The case studies that are shared within the pages of this book are true, but I have taken care to omit any identifying information. All of the names and personal information have been changed in order to protect the identity of those that have so generously shared their stories in this book. Most of these cases occurred in foreign countries. I have lived and worked in four different countries, and worked in many others. I always chose different names for the clients who share their stories, but it is impossible to avoid common names. Never was the real name of the person used. My clients (past and present) can be assured that if they find a case with the same name it is not related to them. Any similarity is pure coincidence. Silvia's story is the sole exception because she specifically asked to be identified.

Many of these stories were written during or shortly after the session. I have tried to maintain the language and expressions of the client. I asked the editor not to correct the grammar in these situations so that the reader can "hear the real voice" of the client.

Finally, the essence of these stories has been maintained in order to illustrate what this new reprocessing therapy can do to improve people's lives. Unfortunately, the emotion and physical expressions are lost in the writing. Even so, we believe the readers will be able to understand how the sessions unfolded, as well as the speed and impact of EMDR therapy.

---

[1] Bergmann, U. (2012) *Neurobiological Foundations for EMDR Practice*. Springer Publishing House.

[2] http://acestoohigh.com/2012/10/03/the-adverse-childhood-experiences-study-the-largest-most-important-public-health-study-you-never-heard-of-began-in-an-obesity-clinic
Retrieved January 4, 2015

About EMDR Therapy[3]

EMDR – Eye Movement Desensitization and Reprocessing - which was discovered in the United States by Dr. Francine Shapiro in 1987. Since then, more than 100,000 therapists have been trained worldwide in EMDR.

If we understand that traumas, nightmares and bad memories of adverse situations are stored in a mal-adaptive form in the brain networks, then we can begin to understand how EMDR can reprocess these fears, phobias, terrors, and anxieties that are connected to painful memories that keep victims trapped by these ghosts from the past. This is accomplished by the integration of reprocessed information that was once in separate parts of the brain. In an accelerated and adaptive manner, EMDR seems to "imitate" what happens to people as they go through the REM (Rapid Eye Movement) phases of the sleep cycle. This is the phase when the brain processes daily life and stores it in an adaptive form, then transforms it into past memory. For reasons that are not totally understood, in some situations people are not able to process this information in a normal and healthy manner. Perhaps this is the origin of nightmares, startle responses, intrusive and obsessive thoughts, or post-traumatic stress disorder (PTSD) and its consequences. In some cases, people can develop Dissociative Identity Disorder (DID) as a result of chronic, repetitive and constant traumas (such as incest) that occur during childhood.

In order to apply EMDR, the psychotherapist needs to have been duly trained in accredited courses, where both EMDR theory as well as the practice of the eight phases of EMDR therapy is taught along with three-pronged (past, present and future) protocol. Trained therapists learn how to evaluate the indication (or lack thereof) for EMDR therapy; how to develop a treatment plan for those cases where EMDR therapy is indicated; and how to conceptualize the diagnosis and treatment according to Adaptive Information Processing (AIP) which is the theoretical basis for EMDR. Beginning with the first phase, the patient shares his or her history, and the therapist then identifies the adverse situations, traumas and painful memories that may become targets for future reprocessing. In the second phase, the therapist will help the patient install positive resources that will help the patient face difficult moments within or outside the sessions. Different kinds of bilateral stimulation (visual, auditory and tactile) are

---

[3] This explanation is taken from a chapter in the author's book, **Healing the Folks Who Live Inside,** volume 1 in the series, *Clinical Strategies in Psychotherapy.*

offered to the patient so that he or she can become familiar with it. In addition, the EMDR approach is explained to the client in order to obtain informed consent. In the third phase we "open" the brain file that contains the difficult memory by asking for the image, beliefs, emotions and sensations that are tied to it.

EMDR therapists use two measurements scales. The first is the SUDS (Subjective Units of Disturbance Scale) which measures disturbance. Therapists will often ask the patient, "On a scale of one to ten, where ten is the greatest disturbance that you can imagine, and zero is no disturbance at all, how much disturbance do you feel when you think about that experience right now?" This allows the therapist to accompany the level of resolution of the experience while the bilateral stimulation is being applied. Joseph Wolpe who worked with desensitization and developed the means to evaluate subjective experiences statistically originally developed this scale.

The therapist also uses a second type of measurement when asking the client to think of an ideal situation in which the present experience has been totally resolved. The therapist then asks, "On a scale of one to seven, where seven is completely true and one is completely false, how true do you feel the positive belief about this experience is to you when you think about it?" Francine Shapiro developed this second scale, making it possible to accompany the resolution of the traumatic experience as it is processed and becomes more and more adaptive in nature.

Because of these measurements, it is possible to develop statistical designs for empirical research. One of Dr. Shapiro's greatest contributions has been her insistence on research which has led to the publication of over 200 scientific studies in peer-reviewed journals, many of which deal with EMDR in the treatment of medically unexplained pain. There now exists journal dedicated specifically to *EMDR Research and Practice*[4]. In 2010, EMDR was recognized and acknowledged as an evidence-based psychotherapeutic approach by the National Registry of Evidence-Based Programs and Practices (NREPP)[5]. Nowadays, EMDR efficacy is undeniable.

In the fourth phase, the therapist applies the bilateral stimulation that helps the brain reprocess the painful and/or traumatic memories. The bilateral stimulation re-activates the Adaptive Information Processing system which was previously unable to fully process the experience and

---

[4] http://www.springerpub.com/product/19333196 retrieved March 16, 2013
[5] http://nrepp.samhsa.gov/ViewIntervention.aspx?id=199 retrieved March 16, 2013

therefore stored the information mal-adaptively. EMDR gives the brain a second chance to reprocess the traumatic memory, thus transforming it into an adaptive resolution.

Oftentimes, people will have intense emotional reactions when reprocessing. This should not surprise us, since past experiences come up much in the same way that they had been stored. This does not mean that the person is being re-traumatized. It simply means that the negative content is being discharged from where they had been originally stored.

On the other hand, intense abreactions can reach a tipping point since it is no longer an issue of reprocessing because the client may dissociate and the processing stops altogether. The person's brain becomes unable to make the adaptive connections necessary to take the experience to an adequate resolution. We can say that with over-the-top emotions, some of the Inner Roles[6] (or inner parts) get scared and "flee" (dissociate again) to their frozen places in order to protect themselves. Through dissociation (a spitting off of certain memories from the main body of awareness or consciousness) they go to the place where they have the illusion of being protected (and pay a high price for this). But the survival strategy once again converts the situation into an ice cage.

Each traumatized role has aspects that are frozen and dissociated. When the client connects to this role, it triggers all that was stored away dysfunctionally. Oftentimes, what is triggered are roles that were frozen in childhood, a time when the person had fewer resources, options or choices regarding how to deal with what was happening to them. Their "emotional circuits" got overloaded and dissociation was how they survived.

The fifth phase begins when the negative and painful memories have been reprocessed, because then positive beliefs can be linked to the target memory the client is working on. It is as if the patient, having emptied out the glass of dirty water, can now fill that glass with clean water.

In the sixth phase, the client does a mental scan of his/her body and determines if there is any physical disturbance left in their body. If there is any left, this is also processed with bilateral stimulation.

The session ends with the seventh phase, in which the client is given specific instructions about what to expect between sessions, how to contact the therapist if necessary, and how to take note of what happens to them during the coming week.

---

[6] For a longer explanation about EMDR and Role Therapy, read the author's book, *Healing the Folks Who Live Inside*, available on Amazon.

Finally, the eighth phase occurs when the client returns for the next session, and the therapist receives his/her feedback and evaluates the results from the previous session. This information will help guide the therapist concerning how to proceed with the treatment plan.

As always, an appropriate history-taking is essential in order to evaluate whether the client is suitable for this kind of psychotherapy, since there can be contra-indications. Although the results can be amazing at times, these are not "miracle cures."

In order to process effectively, it is necessary for the patient to feel safe and secure. A great part of this security comes from the therapeutic relationship. If it is not possible to trust the person who will accompany us on this healing pilgrimage – and there may be terrifying parts on the road – then patient will not surrender to the healing process. After all, there is a whole gallery of roles for whom the Adult feels responsible--roles that need protection. If any of the inner roles don't feel safe and protected, or if they get scared, or feel frightened, the process will not move forward.

This is one of the reasons why we emphasize that what heals is love. Perhaps it sounds strange to talk about love in a psychotherapeutic context, but it is love, positive affect, and unconditional positive regard that will give clients enough security and a sense of safety so they can find the courage to board the ship of hope and stay onboard till the very end. It is the security of unconditional acceptance on the part the therapist that will encourage the patients to take this trip inside of themselves to visit the members of their Inner Gallery[7] (a creative construct that I developed to explain role theory in a simple way). Getting to know the wounded members of their Inner Gallery will allow them to be healed with these new psychotherapeutic tools; but without love, no one has the courage for the trip.

What is it about EMDR that makes it seem like a paradigm shift in psychotherapy? First of all, it is an approach that produces brain changes. Modern brain scans[8] demonstrate the physical changes that result from the application of EMDR. The resolution of the painful experience is the result of the integration of neuronal information that is often dissociated in the brain networks where the traumatic information and the resources for healing are stored in separate hemispheres. Sometimes clients say that they "don't have words to explain what happened", and this is literally true

---

[7] See the author's book, *Healing the Folks Who Live Inside* for a full explanation

[8] Lansing, K., Amen, D., Hanks, C., Rudy, L. (2005) High Resolution Brain SPECT Imaging and EMDR in Police Officers With PTSD. *The Journal of Neuropsychiatry and Clinical Neurosciences* (17) 4.

because the unprocessed memory is dissociated from the part of the brain that can attribute words and meaning to what they have experienced. Only after it is reprocessed can the client report an integrated explanation to their experience.

Secondly, talking about their negative experiences is not necessary for clients to heal. For 120 years psychotherapists have been taught that patients must talk about their painful experiences in order to change (beginning with Breuer's revolutionary "talking cure"). However, with EMDR, talking can be kept to a minimum, since what will heal the patient is the reprocessing of the memory in the brain. For some clients who are shy, or too embarrassed or too ashamed to talk about some of their experiences (such as sexual abuse or rape), this aspect of EMDR is a godsend; it allows clients to reprocess their memories in private.

Perhaps the greatest joy we have as EMDR therapists is to hear our patients, when they have finished reprocessing their memories, tell us things like...

"It's over. Now it's distant. It's in the past."

And when they come back in the following sessions they say:

"I remember, but it doesn't bother me anymore."

"I can't remember it like I did before."

"It's not clear and crisp anymore. The picture is cloudy."

"Is it normal to have so much relief in such a short amount of time?"

"People say and do those things that bothered me so much before, and now, it doesn't matter anymore."

"I'm sleeping well for the first time in years!"

"Hmm, how strange. I haven't thought about that at all during the week."

"Funny, this EMDR stuff... It's like it never happened to me. It's like the EMDR put that experience in a place where it never happened. It's like I used to look at a room filled with old stuff and now it's all gone. Everything is organized and I can't even remember what it was like before!"

"This EMDR is magic...!"

Understanding Pain: An Introduction

There are many factors that contribute to both physical as well as to emotional pain. It is beyond the scope of this book to give a long explanation about an issue that could fill a whole library. However, there are some basic aspects that need to be taken into consideration when treating patients with both kinds of pain.

A medical exam is absolutely essential, preferably by a specialist. There are many pain clinics that are focused primarily on treating pain. Most psychotherapists do not have extensive medical knowledge about physical pain. On the other hand, physicians do not usually take into consideration the psychological and emotional causes of physical pain, especially those experiences from early childhood.

Nowadays, there is a greater understanding of the consequences and sequelae of traumatic events in the lives of people who suffer from physical pain. It is estimated that between 20% to 35% of those who survive a traumatic event go on to develop Post-Traumatic Stress Disorder (PTSD)[9]. Maginn[10] (2013) mentioned the fact that people who have chronic physical pain have symptoms that are very similar to PTSD: anxiety, depression, anger, flashbacks regarding medical procedures they have been through. It is common to develop a drug dependency for medications prescribed to alleviate pain. Family members feel impotent to help a person who is slowly being transformed into somebody else, due to the consequences of chronic pain, of physical and/or emotional origin.

The National Institutes of Health (NIH) in the US estimate that there are more than five million people with a diagnosis of fibromyalgia, a disorder that is still not well understood, but is characterized by deep pain in the tissues, fatigue, headaches, depression and insomnia. A friend of mine received this diagnosis two years after the unexpected and tragic death of her son in a freak accident. She said, "The doctors say that fibromyalgia tends to show up two years after a serious trauma. It seems this is what happened to me after the death of my son. I have never been able to get over what happened."

---

[9] *Living with Pain: PTSD and Chronic Pain*, de Mark Maginn, Retrieved Oct. 11, 2014
[10] http://americannewsreport.com/living-with-pain-ptsd-and-chronic-pain-8817370 Retrieved Oct. 11, 2014

According to Maginn, research show that patients with fibromyalgia can have an increased neural activity in the insula, a region of the brain that is involved in processing pain and emotion. Perhaps this can help us better understand how pain – and emotion - can be affected by inadequate processing in the brain, one of the fundamental theories (AIP – Adaptive Information Processing) of how EMDR therapy works.

Dr. Uri Bergmann[11] (2014) presents a detailed explanation, full of updated research about the new discoveries of neurobiology and how they should guide the practice of psychotherapy. One of his chapters offers an excellent opportunity to understand the neurobiological workings of the brain as well as the adaptive information processing, the organization of memory and consciousness as well as their disorders (dissociative processes). It also expounds on the link between trauma, and physical symptoms and diseases that are not presently explained by medicine, such as rheumatoid arthritis, lupus, Crohn's disease, and Hashimoto's thyroiditis. For those who would like to understand the neurobiological underpinnings of trauma and their connection to physical disease, this is mandatory reading.

One of the most significant and little known studies that also lays the foundation for the traumatic origin of physical diagnoses is the *Adverse Childhood Experiences Study*[12] that lasted 25 years and involved over seventeen thousand participants. It demonstrated that theses adverse childhood experiences were more common in the histories of adults with serious health problems, and illustrated their connection with chronic illnesses and social problems in the United States.

The story of this study begins when Dr. Vincent Felitti became intrigued with what was happening in his obesity clinic in 1985. Half of the persons who sought help abandoned the program precisely when *they were losing a lot of weight*. They left the program when things were going well! He began a review of their medical histories and discovered that all of them were born within a normal weight range. They had not been gaining weight

---

[11] Bergmann, U. (2014) *Neurobiological Foundations for EMDR Practice*. New York: Springer Publishing Company. http://amzn.to/1Ng1xJb

[12]   http://acestoohigh.com/2012/10/03/the-adverse-childhood-experiences-study-the-largest-most-important-public-health-study-you-never-heard-of-began-in-an-obesity-clinic Acessado 4/01/2015

steadily during their childhood years. In fact, they had put on the pounds suddenly, abruptly, and subsequently stabilized at the higher threshold.

Dr. Felitti developed a structured interview with the participants that had left the program in order to try and find out what was happening. At one point, he later realized he had erred when asking one of the formal interview questions, and mistakenly inquired about how much did the participant weigh when she had her first sexual experience. She answered, "Forty-six pounds". He thought she had misunderstood his question, so he repeated it. She confirmed her reply and added, "I was four years old and it was my father," and broke down in tears. That is when he realized what it was that he had asked. Dr. Felitti thought it was sheer madness because in 23 years of medical practice he had come across two cases of incest.

In the following weeks, he began to discover that the majority of the people he was interviewing had a history of childhood sexual abuse, if the question was asked that way. Thinking that perhaps he was asking the questions in an inappropriate manner, he requested that five of his colleagues interview the next 100 participants on the list. The results were the same. Of the 286 people interviewed, almost all of them had histories of childhood sexual abuse.

Another participant helped him put another piece of the puzzle together. She commented that the year after she was raped, she gained 100 pounds. "Being overweight means being invisible, and that's what I needed the most," she said. Suddenly he realized that these people didn't see their weight as a problem, but rather as a *solution.*

Eating calmed their anxiety, in much the same way as alcohol, cigarettes or illicit drugs. Being overweight protected them from rape – because they weren't attractive; from bullying at school – because the kids tended to ignore them; and so on…

Dr. David F. Williamson, an epidemiologist, heard Dr. Felitti present at the prestigious annual conference of the *North American Association for the Study of Obesity.* Most of his colleagues had applauded politely, but thought that these were just more excuses patients thought up to explain their failure to lose weight. With Dr. Williamson it was different. Eventually, these two doctors were joined by Dr. Robert Anda, and in 1995, they put together the study with Kaiser Permanente where 17.421 people were evaluated, according to ten different kinds of childhood adverse experiences.

The results were shocking. Not only did they find the connection between trauma and illness, but also perceived the impact of trauma in the lives of these people. The larger the number of traumas and adverse experiences, the greater risk for getting sick as adults.

First of all, they discovered there was a direct link between trauma in childhood and the beginning of chronic illness in adulthood, the risk of spending time in jail, and work issues, such as absenteeism.

Secondly, they saw that two-thirds of these adults suffered different *kinds* of traumas. For example, someone who had an alcoholic father will probably have suffered verbal or physical abuse as well. Traumas don't happen in isolation.

A third discovery was the link between the high number of adverse childhood experiences and the increased risk for developing serious medical, mental and social problems when adults. The more adverse experiences these people reported, the greater the probability of developing a serious illness in adult life.

This team developed the Adverse Childhood Experiences (ACE) scale to measure the amount of difficult experiences people had in childhood. It is being used in many countries to evaluate the risk of illness in adult life based on the number of adverse childhood experiences that clients report. Here are Portuguese researchers Silva and Maia:

> *Adverse childhood experiences have been described in the literature as one of the principal risk factors for psychosocial problems in adult life. This fact increases the importance of using instruments that permit the evaluations of such occurrences. The Family ACE Questionnaire (Fellitti & Anda, 1998) is a questionnaire that evaluates 10 adverse experiences that may occur in childhood: physical abuse, emotional abuse, sexual abuse, exposure to domestic violence, substance abuse in the home, divorce or parental separation, imprisonment of a family member, mental illness or suicide, physical negligence and emotional negligence. Each of these scales is comprised of several items that can be classified on a likert scale. These scales make it possible to calculate the total adversity that corresponds to the summation of the value with which each subject was classified in each of the categories.*[13]

---

[13] http://hdl.handle.net/1822/11323 Retrieved 25/Jan/2015

This study confirms what many psychotherapists have known empirically: that the origin of symptoms and present illnesses has its origin in the person's past. The EMDR therapy structure is such that the patient is asked to remember the first time a specific issue occurred. The origin of many present-day problems lies in the distant past of the adults in therapy. A recent study[14] confirms that women with Post-Traumatic Stress Disorder (PTSD) are twice as likely to develop diabetes when compared to those without this diagnosis. It becomes easier to understand the importance of taking a good history, especially with an eye to trauma, in the population of patients who have physical pain. Sometimes it can be surprising to find out how it developed, as some of these stories will illustrate.

Finally, since it is very difficult to know where physical pain ends and where emotional pain begins, at times it will be necessary to treat both at the same time. A high level of physical pain drastically reduces the quality of life and creates new problems along the way. Even if people are unable to completely resolve their physical pain, lowering the pain level to a tolerable point brings significant benefits for the client and can translate into better quality of life, with less pain and greater dignity. Installing positive resources that allow the patient to combat chronic disease or better face terminal illnesses helps them to increase their resilience and can decrease depression and hopelessness. It gives them back some sense of control over their situation since they have often dealt with a feeling of enormous impotence about it all. Perceiving treatment as an ally can help establish hope. It brings the perception that maybe cheating their "expiration date" could be possible, in ways that can be very surprising. Guadalupe's story illustrates this.

We believe that EMDR therapy has much to contribute in alleviating the suffering that emerges from the depression, anxiety, fears and phobias regarding illness and pain, especially those aspects that are connected to medical procedures, to physical pain, the consequences of chronic pain or the diagnoses of serious and/or terminal illnesses. The stories we share in this book, along with the clinical strategies that were implemented, offer greater treatment possibilities for diverse situations that are often encountered in the consulting room. By no means is it the last word on this topic, but hopefully through these creative forms of treatment others can replicate strategies that have produced good results and clients can receive new options and renewed hope.

---

[14]PTSD doubles diabetes risk in women.
http://www.sciencedaily.com/releases/2015/01/150107122906.htm Retrieved 8/Jan/2015

Clinical Strategies:
Classical work of EMDR therapy

In this chapter, I will illustrate how the classical work of EMDR therapy can help resolve issues related to physical pain through the use of case studies. In some instances, the pain went away completely, as with Silvia. In other situations, EMDR therapy was an adjunct contribution, like Sawyer's situation.

It has been surprising to see how much physical pain has traumatic origin. Ana, a young adolescent, had strong headaches, but had never connected them to a difficult experience she had had during basketball training. Miranda recovered her independence after a knee surgery that had completely devastated her. In all of the cases in this chapter, the traditional EMDR protocol was enough to bring these clients to a pain resolution in very few sessions. In fact, for some, it resolved in only one session!

Imperceptible traumatic events

Silvia asked to use her real name when it came to sharing about her experience with a bad migraine she struggled with for years. Whenever she sat beneath a strong light, she would immediately develop a splitting headache. It was so notorious that even family members would often point out places for her to sit at restaurants to avoid the bright lights and the subsequent migraine. You can hear how this cleared up in Silvia's own words:

"One day, at a friend's suggestion, I[15] decided to work on an operation I had had recently. I had gotten very ill during a trip and wound up having to have surgery. We presumed correctly that no matter how small a surgery is in general, just the fact of going through surgery is enough to wonder if everything was really all right, or if things wound up "floating around" in the unconscious, like some frozen trauma.

"When the EMDR session began, I was asked what moment of the whole surgical experience had the greatest impact on me. What came up immediately was the scene when I went into the operating room (OR). I confess that up to this point I was just watching and thinking about it, because I really couldn't think of anything in my life that I found disturbing associated to this operation, so much so that the post-op had gone smoothly without incident.

---

[15] Silvia Malamud tells her story here. She is a clinical psychologist, trained in Brief Therapy, and a Certified EMDR Therapist as well as a Brainspotting therapist.

"The therapist set up the EMDR protocol and several scenes came up regarding my entry into the OR. I really found all of this so interesting because I had never had this kind of experience with EMDR before. (It is magnificent the way our creative brains have singular intelligence to process our issues.) As the scenes unfolded I began to have some emotional discomfort. I relived the moment when they gave me the anesthesia and in a flash, I jumped from that scene to another one that really surprised me. Up until that moment it had been totally forgotten. In fact, I didn't even know the experience existed. I saw myself waking up in the middle of a medical procedure. I relived the moment as if it were happening to me right then, even though I knew that wasn't so. I had opened my eyes [when I awoke in the middle of a previous operation] and what I remember is that I was blinded by the overhead lights in the operating room. I was totally awake and aware that the surgery had not ended. I didn't feel any pain. I just woke up to the discomfort of the blinding lights. I remember that a few seconds went by, while I was looking at the lights until the brightness made me nauseous. Confused, I said that I was awake. The doctors and nurses heard me, and without even looking at me, commented amongst themselves that I should be sedated once again. After the surgery, no one made any reference to it. I forgot it and moved forward with my life.

"Up to this point in the EMDR session, with the revelation of what had happened to me, I thought to myself, without any discomfort, 'OK, the session is over... very interesting [as if I were just watching what happened].' However, in the body scan phase of the protocol I still had residual disturbance. So, we went with that!

"All of a sudden, I began to have the migraine symptoms, something I had infrequently. I continued reprocessing. More and more scenes showed up, where I felt my headache triggers. I had never put this together, but the fact is that after the event when I woke up in the OR during surgery, every time I went to some restaurant where there was a ceiling light pointed in my direction, I would ask to change places. The reasons? I would begin to have the subtle symptoms of a migraine headache and nausea. Bingo! This was the remaining piece of discomfort from having awoken during surgery and all that it has meant for me emotionally. The harsh light above my head, plus the focus on me, were directly associated to the moment in the OR when I woke up before surgery was done.

"From this moment on, the reprocessing was completely finished, having gone to extremely freeing places in my brain. The result? It has been three years since that session and I've never had another headache or even the imminent symptoms of one. When I was asked to write this story, even though we had discussed it many times before, I hadn't remembered how much it upset me to keep looking for places to sit in restaurants so that I could avoid strong lights pointed in my direction."

This case illustrates with incredible clarity how certain afflictions, discomforts and pain can have traumatic origins. Waking up in the middle of surgery is everybody's nightmare. In this particular case, the results were migraines that would show up when external circumstances triggered the somatic memory, even though the conscious memory had been lost due to the anesthesia and post-op recovery. Like Silvia said, she had never connected the dots that her headaches had begun after the earlier surgery she had had many years before. Once she remembered, it became obvious why strong lights would trigger the migraines. Perhaps the most surprising aspect was the total resolution of her pain. Silvia never had another migraine again after reprocessing the memory of that surgical incident.

Ana: Headaches

Ana was only 16 years old when she came to therapy to deal with her issues of anxiety and performance. When she was beginning to finalize treatment, she mentioned that she had a persistent headache that was often debilitating. As we discussed the situations in which this would happen, we made the decision to work on the headache. What follows are the notes from the session.

C (Ana): Today I'm doing well, but there are days when I really get a bad headache.

T: Do you remember when this began?

C: I remember that I was about 10-11 years old. It always hurts in the same place, like a pulsating vein. I think, wow, I'm dead. I feel the pain and a lot of stress on my head. When I think about that, it's a six on the scale.

We set up the classic EMDR protocol with this information and began reprocessing.

C: I don't feel any pain, but the scenes where my head hurts came up. I sit down; massage my head. I avoid taking any medication because I don't like to take anything. It takes a while to go away. (BLS[16])

T: If you could imagine some kind of medicine or an antidote that would make the headache go away, what would it be? (BLS)

C: OK, I imagined it... Oh, by the way, something I hadn't remembered before. When I get cold, I get the headache. During the winter, my body is hot even when it's cold outside. (BLS)

C: Now I see myself playing without a headache.

---

[16] (BLS) = Bilateral Stimulation, characteristic of EMDR therapy. They can be visual, auditory or tactile. Unless otherwise mentioned, the therapist used eye movements.

T: And when you think about the words, I can play without pain, how true do you feel these words to be on a scale of one to seven where one is completely false and seven is completely true?

C: Seven.

T: Think about that and follow the movements. (BLS)

C: Hmmm, out of nowhere... I remember that I lost about thirty pounds in two months and the pain intensified. I went on a diet.

T: Think about that. (BLS)

C: OK, now I feel better about the idea that I am going to have a headache forever.

T: Now when you think about these words, I can live without pain, how true do they seem to you now, on a scale of one to seven

C: It's a six.

T: Let's go with that. (BLS)

C: I have some eyesight problems and I need to wear glasses. (BLS) I need to pull out the root of my headache. (BLS)

C: I just remembered... I was going into the fifth grade, and I had never gotten any kind of failing grades. And I had bad grades in French. I was really frightened about it. I kept getting bad grades. To this day I get nervous about it. The school had very high standards. But I always passed. (BLS) Ok. Done.

T: Let's heal the fright? It seems your fear of failure showed up about the same time as your headaches? (BLS)

C: I did better in high school than in grade school, with this fear of failure. On the tests I couldn't connect the answers to the questions. (BLS) I explained it to her, to that ten-year-old. Up until the fourth grade... they didn't prepare us for fourth grade. Now I am on the honor roll. So I explained that to her, to that little girl, that it was the school's mistake, not having prepared us for fourth grade. She understood. She really got it. She wasn't happy about it, but she understood that later on she would be better prepared.

T: So, do you still need to have a headache for that reason? (BLS)

C: No.

T: Then let's tell this little girl that had such a fright that she doesn't need to have a headache about this anymore.

C: All she has to do is study!

T: Now, on a scale of one to seven, when you think about the headache, and the words, I can live without pain, what is it?

C: Seven

T: What are you going to do when the headache tries to show up again?

C: I'm going to take my medicine. I imagined myself having a headache during the week we have tests. I closed my eyes, and I thought: Be calm, breathe, get a glass of water, and then we can go back to the books... and it got better. Now I have my own medicine. And it works really well!

T: So, now when you think about the original incident, the one we started with, on a scale of zero to ten, how much does it bother you now?

C: Zero.

C: I can use my medicine whenever I need to. All of this has been really interesting. Now it's over. Gone. I don't have any marks left, nothing.

T: And now, when you think about all of this, and scan your body - do you feel any disturbance?

C: No. It's done.

T: Then let's stop here for today. As you know, the processing often continues after the session is over. If you need anything, give me a ring, ok?

Comments:

Ana was already very familiar with strategies of working with the "Inner Gallery of Roles[17], a creative construct that I developed to explain role theory in a simple way. All of us have inner roles that are not healed and that often behave in childlike/childish ways, depending on the age at which the difficult or traumatic event occurred. In this case, Ana already knew that she needed to help this younger role that was frightened at age ten. So her (more) Adult role went into action. And helped explain things to the younger role. Perhaps this is one of the most efficient ways of repairing memories of situations and relationships in the past that affected people in their childhood and adolescence.

A few years later, in a follow-up contact, Ana commented that the painful headache crises had greatly improved. They tended to show up when she gets stressed out, but that she takes a deep breath, takes her medicine, and it quickly goes away... adult behavior.

Guadalupe: overcoming cancer

Guadalupe had had a series of illnesses before she came to therapy. She talked about how difficult it had been to deal with her husband's family, with her mother who lived with them in order to help her with the family and chores, due to Guadalupe's own physical limitations. We spent many sessions working on Guadalupe's bitterness and resentments, especially with regard to her husband's family, and slowly Guadalupe began to lighten up.

One day she came in very nervous and frightened. When I asked her what was going on she replied:

---

[17] For greater details about this, read, *Healing the Folks Who Live Inside,* by the same author, available on Amazon.

25

"As you know, I had ovarian cancer some 2-3 years ago. The doctors operated thinking that it was a benign nodule, and during surgery realized it was cancer. Since then, I always do my medical check-ups. The doctor told me last week that if my numbers continue to go up that I would have to face chemotherapy again! To be honest, I don't know if I am more afraid of the cancer or of the chemo! I am so frightened! I don't want to lose my hair again and go through all of the side effects of all that. Is there something we can do?"

I remembered I had read a book by Bernie Siegel many years ago, *Love, Medicine and Miracles*[18]. In it he described how he worked with his cancer patients. He discovered that 5% of them did not die even though the medical prognosis was the worst possible, and others lived years beyond any life expectancy for their illness. When he studied these "exceptional" patients, he found that they had made significant changes in their lives and lifestyle. Over time, he studied the relationship of these patients with their treatment. He would ask them to draw a picture of how they perceived going through chemotherapy, and for those of his patients that saw it as something that would poison them, he would research alternative treatment (radiation). If no other alternatives were available he would work with the patient in order to change their perception of chemotherapy so that they could see it as an ally in becoming healthy again. I vividly remember to this day the author's description of a patient who visualized his immune system as if it were a "Pac-man[19] that would "gobble up" the cancer cells and eliminate them. It had excellent results. So I decided to try something similar with Guadalupe, but this time with EMDR therapy.

I told her about the book and the exercise, and she liked the idea. Using slow bilateral movements we installed the pictures in her imagination. I asked Guadalupe to imagine her immune system as these agents that could devour the cancer cells in her body. She was very religious (Catholic) and commented afterwards that it was like the Holy Spirit was going through her body, illuminating it and making the cancer cells show up so the killer agents could destroy the malignant cells. Then her body could expel them.

After a few weeks, Guadalupe interrupted treatment because her husband lost his job and she could no longer afford to come to therapy. I was really concerned about her situation.

A year later, she came back. I noticed she still had her hair as we sat down and thought to myself, *"Well, she doesn't look like she went through chemo."* Guadalupe shared that she had gone through a very difficult period. Her mother had passed away and so the care of her children and of the

---

[18] **Siegel, Bernie S. (2011)** *Love, Medicine and Miracles*. **William Morrow Paperbacks**
[19] An Atari® video game.

household was now all squarely on her shoulders. But I was really amazed when I asked about her medical issues.

"*Oh, I never had anything anymore. The numbers started going down and I never had to do chemotherapy.*" When I asked her what had happened and to what did she attribute her obvious improvement, she explained to me that she had done the Pac-man exercise religiously.

"*Every day, before I got out of bed and before I went to sleep, I did that exercise that you taught me here. And sometimes if I had a free moment, I would do it some more. I would scan my body and kill off whatever cancer cells there were. So my numbers started going down. I got out of having to do chemo!! You know, "doctorita", I'm kind of afraid to say this out loud, but I think I'm cured of the cancer.*"

Guadalupe was obviously ecstatic and I rejoiced with her. I had an edge of concern about her optimism because I knew that ovarian cancer was usually so lethal although not one of the most common cancers. Hers had not been an easy challenge.

A year later, Guadalupe ended therapy. I stayed in touch with the medical doctor who had referred her to me. Every once in a while, I would ask her about Guadalupe and she would tell me she was fine. Nine years later, I met up personally with Guadalupe and she was in total remission, considered truly cured of the cancer. It has been fifteen years now since we did that exercise and she continues healthy and without any relapses.

Clinical Strategies:
Drawing protocol applied to pain issues

Having patients draw pictures of their pain gives enormous insight to both client and therapist. I was originally trained in Psychodrama where I used drawings extensively. So it was natural to use them in EMDR therapy. Eventually I even developed a specific protocol for adult use of drawings with EMDR therapy[20]. But it was when I saw Mark, an EMDR pain specialist, Grant ask his clients for pictures of their pain that I realized the richness of using them with clients who have pain issues. It also serves the purpose of comparison when used as pre- and post-EMDR sessions, allowing both therapist and client to "see" what is happening inside.

Lucia

Lucia commented during her session that she had always had digestion problems. As an adult, she found out that she had been born with extra inches in her intestines, and that this slowed down her whole digestive process. Everything was more complicated. She mentioned that she was afraid that one day her "guts would tie into a knot". We used this expression of her fears and I asked her to draw a picture of how she perceived her physical situation. This is what she drew:

We set up the drawing protocol, using the picture of her pain she had drawn as the image; the expression, "my guts are tied in a knot" as the negative belief about herself, and she mentioned her feelings of frustration, anguish and even anger at her "factory defect". We went into the reprocessing phase, and both of us were totally surprised when she recovered a childhood memory.

---

[20] **The EMDR Drawing Protocol for Adults,** *in* EMDR *Scripted Protocols*, edited by Luber, M., New York: Springer Publishing company, 2009, p 107-109.

"Look at what I remembered! When I was seven years old, on a Tuesday afternoon, my grandmother came over to our house. Along with my mother, they grabbed me and laid me down, spread-eagle, while one of them placed a suppository to help me go to the bathroom! It has been years since I thought about that!"

We continued reprocessing the scene until her disturbance went to zero. Then I asked her to make a second drawing, about how she perceived herself now.

"Now I have the feeling that the way out is clear, so my digestion can work comfortably. I feel normal. It doesn't matter that I have these extra inches. This is the way I am and that's OK."

We connected this positive belief that had emerged from the memory with the new drawing, and checked for any bodily disturbances. Lucia left the session very satisfied, happy that she had been able to work on this old issue that had bothered her for so long.

In the following session, she shared a very interesting observation. *"You know, all of my life I've had this strange feeling in my anus, that things were going in instead of coming out. After we reprocessed that memory in the last session, the feeling vanished! Gone! It was incredible! That uncomfortable feeling is completely gone. Now I really know I'm normal!"*

Some observations about Lucia's experience are in order. First of all, it is interesting to see how traumatic memory holds such explicit detail. She even remembered *the day of the week* when it had happened! Traumatic memory is quite different from normal memory, since the brain doesn't have to file away routine and unnecessary information in order to survive. In traumatic memory, unprocessed information will often reappear in rich detail, even with memories that had been apparently forgotten.

Another point has to do with the traumatic origin of somatic memory. We see this happen over and over again when we work with patients who have pain issues. This should alert us to the fact that there are physical diagnoses that may improve significantly after EMDR treatment. The difficult part is knowing when the origin is traumatic since so often the person doesn't remember the incident that may have given way to the physical symptom, as we saw here with Lucia. However, EMDR therapy can be pretty efficient in bringing up these lost memories, as we saw in this case.

Sawyer

Sawyer had been diagnosed HIV positive six years before we met. We were investigating the possibility of strengthening his immune system with EMDR therapy so that he could avoid going on medication. On one hand it would help combat the effects of his illness, but on the other there were side effects he didn't want to face if possible. Sawyer wanted to postpone as much as possible his use of medication. His doctor agreed with him this far because his viral count was so low; but due to a series of serious stressors he had been going through, his CD4 count (used to indicate how his immune system was responding adequately to the virus) had gone down significantly. It was now in 250 and the doctor alerted him that if it hit 200 he would have to go on the medication. Sawyer was very fearful about that.

I remembered how I had worked with Guadalupe and the good results we had had with her, so it occurred to me that we could use drawings along with his creative imagination to install some positive resources to help strengthen his immune system. Maybe we could help him use his innate resources to fight off the virus...?

I asked Sawyer to make a drawing of how he felt at that moment about his struggle with the disease. After he had drawn it, he said, *"I feel like I'm detonated. It used to be that I could protect myself from the virus, but now even my shield has shrunk! The viruses are coming at me at a higher speed than I can't defend myself from them. I'm sweating buckets with the effort"*.

Since we wanted to work on his positive resources that might help him face his situation, I also asked him to draw a picture of how he would like to see himself in this struggle.

"I used to feel protected, as if I were under a glass dome. The viruses would hit the glass and crack in half, so I had less and less viruses, at least, that's the way I thought. As a result of this I had always managed to keep my CD4 from dropping too low. But now, with all the crises I've been facing lately, I have trouble seeing myself as I did before."

Sawyer made a new drawing where he was under the glass dome, attacked by the virus, but under protection. On the bottom right hand corner he pointed out the virus that had cracked in half when it touched the glass dome.

We moved on to the second drawing, which was the target of this session. With slow bilateral movements, we installed this positive resource so that he could feel good about the situation. The idea was that Sawyer could have recourse to the image several times a day to send positive thoughts to his body.

When he felt that the resource was strong and accessible, I proposed something else to him. Sawyer was a Christian and he had mentioned that in his church someone had given him a prophetic word that Jesus would purify Sawyer's blood. It is important to respect clients' beliefs and when possible, use them to their advantage, especially if they will help them face serious illnesses and diagnoses. So I said to him:

"Sawyer, you had mentioned earlier that there was a lady at your church that had said that Jesus would purify your blood. What would this look like? Can you draw that?"

Sawyer came out of a nursing background and drew a picture of a blood transfusion.

"OK. I see it like a great blood transfusion. My blood leaves my body, goes to heaven, Jesus cleans out all of the viruses, and when my blood goes back into my body, it returns without the virus. That way I have less and less viruses in my system."

We strengthened these positive pictures with a few more slow bilateral movements, and at the end of the session I gave him my "prescription":

"Sawyer, I would like for you to "take my medicine" every day, at least three times a day, every day. Go over these positive pictures for a few minutes every day. I don't know if it will work. There is no guarantee, but it certainly won't hurt. The important thing here is consistency, to remember to do it every day. Let's see what happens." He agreed and we ended the session.

Sawyer went back to his country of origin and I lost track of him. A year later, he turned up asking to work on something else. Dying of curiosity, I asked him how his health was doing. Sawyer smiled.

"Last week I did my tests once again. My CD4 was at 590! Ever since I was diagnosed I have never had such a high count! My doctor was amazed. She said, 'I don't know what you are doing, but keep doing it because it is working.' I haven't had to start medication and my viral count continues low."

"And to what do you attribute this improvement?"

"Esly, for the first three months after that session we did together, I took "your medicine" every day, religiously. Wherever I was, several times a day, I would remember the pictures and think positive thoughts about them. After a while, I started forgetting to do it, but I can tell that the effect continued. That was it!"

Eight years later, I tracked him down when I began writing this book. (Yeah, Facebook!) I asked him for an update about his condition. He told me that four years earlier, he had faced another very serious crisis. *"This time, I wasn't able to keep it together"*. His defenses had gone down. He and the doctor reached the conclusion that it was time to start medication as a preventive measure.

"I started the medication as a form of protection eleven years after my initial diagnosis. To this day, I don't feel a thing. My defense system is doing well and with the medication my viral count is undetectable, which is just great! I don't have any side effects, nothing. Not even a fingernail hurts! When I go to the hospital for my check-ups, the medical staff thinks I gave them a wrong number because it is so old. I didn't have any trouble taking the medication on a daily basis. It is quite manageable: one pill in the morning and two at night and that's it! Every day, and I have none of the side effects that I feared.

When I asked him if he still "took my medicine", he answered:

"Yes, I do, but not as frequently. My tendency is to do the exercises when I am feeling well. At this point, I'm dealing well with my illness. Life goes on as usual, so much so that my close friends who know about my diagnosis joke about it with me. They say I don't really have anything at all!" And Sawyer let out peals of laughter.

Fifteen years after his initial diagnosis, Sawyer deals comfortably with his illness. He takes his medication, follows medical guidelines and leads a fairly normal life.

Here we see the power of positive installations. We don't presume to say that everyone will have the same results. We have only anecdotal experiences. But the results were very impressive and inspire us to keep working this way with others. Obviously, clients should continue to take their medication and follow doctor's orders. But we hope this case study will serve as an example of one more tool in our kit to help us help others, especially those with chronic illnesses where the immune system plays a part.

Daisy: the hole in my head

I went see Daisy at her house, when she was recovering from a very delicate operation and was housebound. She had recently found out that the drip from her nose was brain fluid, due to the fact that there had been deterioration in the bone structure between her face and brain. The doctors had done a bone graft that required that she stay lying down without raising her head in order to assure a successful result. Once again, we used the opportunity to do resource installation in order to help her with a complete recovery.

Daisy drew the picture below that portrays how she was feeling about all of this, and commented that she had a "hole in her head".

Taking into consideration her negative comment, I asked her to draw another picture of how she would like for the situation to finalize, if her surgery were successful. She drew another picture and commented, "My head is completely sealed."

We started processing the events surrounding the surgery:

- when she first found out that this was a very serious problem seeing that she was dripping brain fluid through her nose;
- that if the opening between her face and brain didn't close well she could risk having a mundane infection go to her brain. Even a cold could cause a brain inflammation that might leave to grave consequences or death;
- the fear and anguish while she waited to see if the graft "took";
- the boredom of having to stay absolutely lying down, according to doctor's orders.

After several series of bilateral movements (tactile, in this case, for obvious reasons), Daisy felt better, and with 15 minutes of reprocessing, her anguish was gone. She was left with a sense of expectancy while she waited, but trusting the graft would "take".

Going back to the positive picture, she said, *"Now it's a bit different. When you asked me on a scale of one to seven how much I believed it was true that my head was sealed, it was like I "saw" the number seven on my head. For me, this number represents perfection, completeness, so I feel like my head is completely healed."*

I asked Daisy to draw a picture of how she perceived this new picture, and we strengthened it as well, as a resource. Once again, I insisted that she do the visualizations several times a day to instruct her body in how it could help heal itself.

Some time later, Daisy's husband got in touch with me to thank me. He commented that she had had a full recovery. That the graft had taken, she was out of danger, and although the recovery process was tiresome, she believed that our session had been helpful in facing things in a positive fashion.

Sandra

This transcription of an EMDR session shows how it can be used as intervention for physical pain. It is possible to perceive the link with painful memories of the past, regarding both the accident itself as well as memories associated to it within the neural networks. EMDR therapy eliminated the pain during this session, and 24 hours later, the patient was still pain-free.

Presenting issue in this session:

About a year before this session took place, Sandra, had suffered an injury to her elbow while doing some exercises. When she went to the doctor, he suggested an infiltration, which he performed. Sandra complained that it was done in such a painful manner that she felt like something had been done wrong, since it seemed to have reached her nerve. With time, the elbow did improve, but eventually the pain returned and in spite of medication, the pain persisted.

She sought out a second opinion and this doctor suggested an infiltration as well, which was been performed two days before this session.

Sandra felt that it had been "done right" this time, but even so, she still had a lot of pain in her elbow and couldn't move her arm freely. She was unable to perform simple tasks like brushing her teeth, or using tableware to eat, etc. She said she felt worse after treatment than before.

She mentioned that she had regretted having done the second infiltration when she did, because she had important commitments for the following days and was limited in her ability to carry out her normal duties. She was in a lot of anguish because the doctor had mentioned the possibility of surgery if the pain persisted. Her anxiety had increased because her pain was getting worse and worse, and she had a great sense of incapacity as a result of it.

In this session, the therapist asked Sandra to draw her pain on a piece of paper. This would serve as her target image.

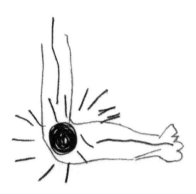

T: When you look at this picture, what words best describe what you think about yourself that are negative?

C: Incapable, or incapable of being healthy

T: Can we use "I'm incapable"? or "I'm incapable of being healthy"?

C: I'm incapable of being healthy.

T: And when you look at this picture again, what are the words that you would like to think about yourself that are positive?

C: I'm free of pain. I'm healthy. The better one is, I'm free of pain.

T: I'm wondering about that cognition, because I don't think it is realistic to believe that people will never have pain again?

C: I feel healthy. I can be healthy.

T: When you think about that, on a scale of one to seven, where seven is completely true and one is completely false, how true do you feel are the words, "I can be healthy"?

C: Seven.

T: And when you think about this experience, and the words, "I'm incapable of being healthy", what emotions come up for you?

C: Deep sadness.

T: And on a scale of zero to ten where ten is the worse disturbance you can imagine and zero is no disturbance at all, how much does it bother you when you think about this?

C: Eight.

T: And where do you feel that in your body?

C: In my arm, my elbow.

T: (The therapist gives appropriate instructions for the desensitization phase, and begins the eye movements.).

C: My heartbeat took off. I'm sweating a lot.

T: (Bilateral Movements = BLS)

C: I had a clear sense... my mother died of cancer, in a lot of pain. She became dependent, with limited capacity to do things. The greatest pain had to do with the pain she felt.

T: (BLS)

C: I always tried to put myself in her place, to feel what she felt, even at the moment of her death. I tried to gain a dimension of her pain. Maybe I somaticized some.

T: (BLS)

C: I ran away quickly to my safe place, put my foot in the water there, at the waterfall, and came back. For my mother, the worst was her limitation; more than her pain. For me, too... to lose my autonomy; to have to ask for help. There's an identification with her. The pain is more bearable than the limitation, the incapacity to do things.

T: (BLS)

C: I'm feeling calmer. I'm not sweating so much. I still feel some pain, a little bit, but I'm not as sad. I have a lesser desire to cry.

T: On a scale of zero to ten, how much does it bother you now?

C: Six.

T: What does the six mean?

C: The feeling of pain is more distant now, but the incapacity isn't. It's like something from the remote past

T: [The therapist continues with the eye movements. When she comes to the end of the set, she asks the client:] Sandra, do you have cancer?

C: No. No! Of course not! (Pause as Sandra thinks.) Now I remember that last week, I was doing extremely well. I was happy, energized. I felt like doing things. I hadn't felt like that in years. It was a wonderful week. I felt good, in spite of the pain. I did everything I needed to do. Then, on Thursday I did the infiltration again. I don't want to blame myself, but I think it was a wrong decision.

T: (BLS)

C: It was like some kind of boycott, a big one. I was doing so well, and I used this elbow to boycott myself. It was the first time I had felt so good since my mother's death four years ago.

T: (BLS)

C: Now I saw a picture, kind of like with special effects from the movies. It's my mother's pain, not mine.

T: (BLS)

C: I remembered several scenes with her; and a photograph I have of her where she's smiling. My daughter is in her lap. My daughter is cross-eyed in it, but it doesn't matter. The important thing is that my mother is smiling. It was rare to see her smile…

T: (BLS)

C: I laugh more than she [mother] does. I have the ability to laugh more than her, and perhaps to be healthier.

T: (BLS)

C: A lot of things came up. I was able to be well last week, in spite of the pain. I was able to enjoy myself, have fun in spite of it. I thought I needed to be absolutely without pain in order to be happy. Pain doesn't have to ruin my life.

T: Do you have a right to be happy now that your mother is dead?

C: I have always had that right. I'm sorry I wasn't able to help her more. She didn't ask for help. She wasn't cured. It was difficult to see her incapacity as something so real, but it is hers, not mine.

T: (BLS)

C: I left her a bit [mother] and thought about my daughters and how they do so well when I am well. I can change this story. It doesn't have to repeat itself.

T: (BLS)

C: I made the wrong decision when I had the infiltration done before this course. My mother also made bad decisions about her illness. I don't have to cry any longer because of this decision. It doesn't have to perpetuate itself. I'm here, not in bed. I'm OK.

T: You have the tools and resources to take better care of yourself than your mother did.

C: The phrase that comes to me is, "This body belongs to me and I can take care of it or not."

T: (BLS)

C: Her body didn't seem to belong to her... now several pleasant memories came up for me. Dancing... the feeling that my body belongs to me.

T: So, what is your decision? Are you or are you not going to take care of yourself?

C: I'm going to care for myself! I don't have to stop living, or stop having joy in order to care for myself. I see myself doing physiotherapy in the afternoon and going out at night to dance.

T: We can stop here or else, go a bit further. I have the impression that you need to repair a few things with your body. I would like to propose that you have a little conversation with your elbow.

C: Here, let me take this off [and she unwraps the bandages from her arm].

[Therapist waits while she takes it off, and then continues eye movements, and asks her to imagine this conversation with her elbow.]

C: I asked it, "Why did you did this to me? Why did you betray me? Why didn't you give me a tip about this?" I think this elbow got misunderstood. I think I wasn't listening to it. Wow, I don't feel any pain right now! [And looks at her arm in amazement].

T: Well, then, let's hear what your elbow has to say to you now. (BLS)

C: What came to mind was something very small. The answer is, "you didn't take care of me." Affection, warmth. I'm so amazed with the lack of pain right now! I think that's what my elbow needed.

T: I would like to know if you and your elbow are playing on the same team?

C: I am going to make that proposal to it.

T: (BLS)

C: The answer didn't come in words. Rather it was a scene: I saw myself dancing to the song, I feel good. I saw myself dancing to the music.

T: Now I have another proposal for you. How about we pay the first doctor a visit?

C: I feel like beating him up!

T: (BLS)

C: Wow, I said a whole bunch of things to him. He wasn't careful. I felt like slapping him with this arm. The first injury was the result of a boxing class. I saw myself playing this videogame, and the doll was the doctor.

T: And now, how much does it bother you, zero to ten?

C: The scene doesn't bother me anymore. Zero. I don't feel any pain. I'm crying from happiness! It had been a long time since I felt like this! [and dries her tears].

T: I would like for you to make a new drawing of yourself now, and the issue of your pain.

C: I'm trembling [and draws the picture with the injured arm].

T: When you look at this drawing now. What do you think about yourself that is positive?

C: I'm happy, joyful, light.

T: So what are we going to install now?

C: I am capable of living without pain.

T: When you think about that now, on a scale of one to seven, where one is completely false and seven is completely true how true do you feel these words are for you now?

C: Now? Seven. I'm not feeling anything [regarding the pain].

T: OK, let's strengthen that. Think about this picture, and the phrase, "I am capable of living without pain"[and the therapists starts the eye movements].

C: I am capable of living without pain. It's done.

T: Think about these positive words, and tell me if there is any disturbance now.

C: Nothing. Not any disturbance. Look! My arm! I can stretch it out! OK, I'm not going to go hunting down for disturbance. It's been hurt. I'm going to take care of it.

End of first session for pain treatment.

Sandra came back on the following day.

T: So, how have you been?

C: I can't believe it! I think it was the medicine. I'm still without pain. I think my body allowed the medicine to take effect now that it got rid of the other stuff. I felt the chemistry of it.

T: And now, on a scale of zero to ten, what is the level of disturbance you have now when you think about it?

C: I'm reluctant to say zero; because I'm still mad at the doctor. Let's say a two.

T: And what would zero look like?

C: Zero is forgetting; no longer being angry. Where it doesn't bother me anymore. I'm still mad. I want it to become a fact, without being impregnated with emotion.

T: And the pain, zero to ten?

C: Zero.

T: Would you like to make an attempt to zero the anger?

C: Ok. At this point, I'm all in favor of things that work! [And smiles.]

T: Think about the anger [therapist starts a few more eye movements].

C: I thought about several things. First, I realized that I had put the healing responsibility in the doctor's hands, and forgot that part of that process belongs to me. I'm mad at him, but also at myself for not accessing my self-cure. It was a mistake. Everyone makes mistakes. Unfortunately, it happened with me. I don't feel like beating him up anymore. It lost its importance. I wouldn't recommend him to anyone, but I'm not going to let that memory continue to occupy space on my hard drive.

T: Let's have a look at your hard drive. How do you want to arrange things in order for us to end the session?

C: A phrase came to mind. Illnesses will always turn up. I may get sick or hurt again. We're subject to that kind of thing. But I can come out of it, and quit feeling pain as well.

T: Let's go back to the scene with the doctor. Now how much does it bother you zero to ten?

C: Zero.

T: *I can quit feeling pain*, one to seven. How true is that now?

C: Seven.

End of follow-up session.

Comments and observations:

This session shows how EMDR can make positive interventions regarding pain issues. The application of the classic eight steps of EMDR therapy, along with a few additional clinical strategies, allowed the pain to go away. It was still gone the next day.

A few observations with regard to the additional interventions are in order.

1. Sandra made an almost immediate connection between her own pain and her mother's pain, illness and her death. When I asked Sandra if she had cancer (a cognitive interweave), the idea was to help Sandra differentiate between her own pain and that of her mother's. This resulted in Sandra being able to express that there was a pain that belonged to her mother and not to herself, Sandra. As a result, Sandra was able to give herself permission to be happy even after her mother's passing away.

2. When the therapist asked Sandra to repair the relationship with her elbow, the idea was to help her incorporate her arm into her body. There was a sense that her arm was somehow dissociated from the rest of her body, and using the bilateral movements, it was possible to achieve this integration. She promised to care for her elbow and left the session "dancing"...

3. Having the patient meet up with the first doctor – with whom she was still very angry – was important so that the memory could be desensitized. It was one of the triggers that could make her pain come back if it wasn't properly resolved.

4. In the follow-up session, one sees how processing occurred outside of the session. Sandra brings back her understanding that the EMDR therapy had allowed the medication to do its job, and eliminated the pain. It was her way of re-signifying what had happened in the previous session.

Role-reversal: Interviewing the body

I believe that the "precious gem" of Psychodrama has always been role-reversal. If Jacob Moreno, the medical doctor who developed Psychodrama and Sociometry, had not done anything else except teach us to work with role-reversal, it would have been enough. There is nothing that compares to it when it comes to understanding another role, be it person, thing or concept.

Now that we have a greater knowledge about the brain and its connections, we can perceive why it is that neurobiologically we are able to have insight into another person or even internal roles of our own (the "inner Gallery of Roles[21]. This happens at such an unconscious level that only when we access these neuronetworks through role-reversal do we perceive how much we really know. Sometimes there are amazing surprises! We are totally unaware of how much we know until we put ourselves into another's shoes (or roles).

Role-reversal allows us to not only reverse with other people, but also with other things, places, feelings, and sensations. We can also role-reverse with our pain, joy, rage or desire for vengeance. The limit is an individual's creativity (or that of the therapist!)

How do we do this?

We can ask the person to come out of their present role ("who they are right now") and take on the role of another person, thing or feeling. For example, we can instruct a client like this:

"I would like for you to stop being Jane for a few moments, and be your son, John. Speak as if you were him. I am going to ask you a few questions, as if I were a reporter, and I would like for you to answer me as if you were John." We can ask Jane to change seats in order to make it clear that this is a different role. If Jane begins to answer as Jane, insist on speaking with "John", in order to keep Jane in John's role.

Then we ask some questions:
- What's your name? How old are you?
- What are you like?
- How did you come into so-and-so's life?

These questions are especially useful when we are interviewing pain or feeling roles.
- What are you doing in … (Jane's) life?

---

[21] See the author's book, _Healing the Folks Who Live Inside_, for a longer explanation for this concept.

- What would you like to say to her? What do you do to her?

- What would need to happen in order to resolve this situation? (This is the "million-dollar question", because we can see if in the other's role they can give us the solution to what is going on.)

- What changes would need to happen in order for this situation to have a good resolution? It is amazing to see how oftentimes in the other role our clients can give us the solution they need and couldn't see before.

Once I did an exercise with a Psychodrama group full of university students. One of the students was presenting the different roles in her life, and nothing seemed to be out of place... until she role-reversed into her father's role.

"Mr. Smith, what do you think about your daughter?" I asked the young woman in her father's role.

"Well, I'm really concerned about her. She had a boyfriend who passed away when she was 15. Ever since then, she's never had a boyfriend again. Not even a date! I really want her to get married, have children, a family. She's already 28 years old. My hunch is she never got over his death. He lived in a different country, and she wanted to go and say goodbye to him, since we knew he was terminal. But you know how it is. In our culture, a young girl like that can't travel alone. And we didn't have the money for her mother to accompany her. So, that's what happened. He passed away, and she stayed here. It was all very sad, but there just wasn't a lot we could do about it. Ever since then, she's never had another boyfriend."

See how this young woman gives us valuable information about an unresolved relationship that had never come up while she was presenting her life roles? When she reversed back into her own role as a university student, we gave her the chance to set up the scene where she was finally able to say goodbye to the young boyfriend. She was able to tell him how much he meant to her, how important he had been, and finally bring closure to this relationship. It was a way for her to be able to eventually open up to new romantic possibilities.

When we add the reprocessing therapy protocols to situations like these, we greatly increase the healing experience. Besides a better understanding of what is happening, we often find the solution, the way out of a lot of problems. And all of this is changing at the brain level: irreversible neurochemical transformations.

When dealing with pain, we can ask the patient to role-reverse with their pain, and explore with them in order to find out what is happening. If we can interview the pain through role-reversal, oftentimes it is possible to find an entry point for the protocol and reprocess in role-reversal. That may be where the resolution for symptom resolution lies.

Once the client is in the role of his or her pain, one can interview the "Pain":

- When did you start? What was she (patient) doing at the time? What was happening in her life?
- What are you doing in their life now?
- What are you doing to him?
- What kinds of things do you say to her?
- What "opened the door" for you to come into their life?
- What makes it possible for you to continue to inflict so much pain on him?
- What needs to happen for you to go away? Is that possible?

Sometimes the replies may give us an indication if the person (and their body) believes that the origin/solution is medical and/or emotional. Any information will help us. What is emotionally based can be reprocessed and should influence the physical symptoms as well.

There are situations where the person doesn't remember when it was that the pain began, but the brain has it filed away, as we saw with Silvia. Our brain stores everything from conception, even if it is only after 24 months of life that the cognitive/verbal aspects kick in and develop. Up until then, memory is mainly somatic, in the body.

EMDR therapy is a tool that can help us access and process these memories. This is especially useful if the memory is traumatic. It is not a therapy aimed specifically at regression, since the intent is not to make the patient remember what was forgotten. However, forgotten memories are often retrieved for reprocessing by the brain, if they were filed away together in the brain's inimitable style of storage. Sometimes the patient isn't even aware of what happened or never had a cognitive memory of it. But the brain can "pull the thread" of connected memories within the same brain file so that it can be reprocessed.

It is worth mentioning that a person who is living with a pain of "ten" on a SUDS scale from zero to ten where ten is the greatest pain imaginable has no quality of life. If we can reprocess the emotional aspects of the pain, it may be possible to decrease the intensity or severity of it, even if some of it remains due to the physical aspects of it. This can make a difference in restoring a new level of quality of life. One can live tolerably well with a pain of "three"(and a few painkillers).

Using role-reversal with a symptom – in this case Pain - is illustrated in detail in the following session. It was recorded during a workshop at the II EMDR Ibero-American Conference in Quito, Ecuador (2010).[22] Since this was a public workshop instead of working with someone's pain, we worked through the structure of case supervision. Several therapists shared about tough cases they were facing, and the group voted for one that they felt would give them the greatest learning experience. The recording has been transcribed with minor editing for readability purposes.

C: I'm Grace's therapist.

T: Say your name again... Yolanda?

C: My name is Yolanda. Grace is 35 years old. She has a lot of physical pain. We're not sure where it all comes from... maybe it is fibromyalgia or maybe it is something else. We are looking for the origin of her pain. During her first three sessions she revealed that her brother, who was later shot to death, had abused her. It seems be a generational issue, because her mother was abused as well and considered it as something normal. No one gave Grace any support.

T: The mother?

C: And the father. They both knew about it, but...

T: About Grace's abuse or the mother's?

C: Grace's abuse. The mother acted like it was no big deal. "I was abused, too. That's life", she said. The father acts like he doesn't care. "He's your brother and you can't do anything about it. You just have to accept it." That bothered her a lot. She's now married and recently decided to separate from her husband. That's why she hasn't come to therapy for a while. We'll have just a short period of time together because she's moving to a different state. I'll be able to work with her for about two months and then she leaves. So, I feel pressured, because I don't know how to deal with all of this, how to help her and give her resources for the future.

Another thing that came up is that she revealed that she grew up in spiritism. Although she says it helps her, she also fears it. She says that she's leaving her marriage because her husband abuses everyone. She made the decision, rather impulsively it seemed to me. One day she came to me and said, "I'm moving to another state... I'm moving on such–and–such a date. I can't take it anymore." She explained that during therapy she would always try to see her husband's side of things. "Ah, he doesn't give me any support, but I understand him. It was better that I did things that way." She never said anything negative about him. Until this last session, when she told me she was experiencing severe physical pain. And that she couldn't take it anymore.

---

[22] This video recording, with English subtitles is available at
www.plazacounselingservices.com

T: Well, you mentioned something about her pain. You said you had made a drawing and mapped out Grace's pain. Tell me a little bit about that.

C: When she comes to the office she comes with a lot of pain... I brought a map of the human body where she could point out where in the body the pain is. There wasn't one part of the body that wasn't hurting. I also told her to add whatever she wanted. She put a kind of protection over the entire body and painted a shadow. She said that this shadow is with her all the time. It never leaves her. Sometimes, when we were reprocessing the pain, she would go to her safe place, a peaceful place. And then we would try and identify the pain. She also drew a picture of the pain and the picture has been changing. It used to be like a red ball with a lot of black spots and scratches. Now sometimes it gets smaller during the session. And there are times when she comes with a lot of anger, with a lot of pain to the sessions; she is angry at the entire world. She herself said, "I have no friends. I hate people. I hate everybody. And I hate myself."

T: Ok. So, Yolanda, I'm going ask you to do an exercise in role-reversal. But instead of becoming Grace, your patient, I want you to become Grace's pain. Ok? (Pause while Yolanda becomes Grace's Pain.) Very well. Now you are Grace's Pain, right? I'd like to ask you to step aside for a few moments. This is a place where you feel no pain. Can you imagine that?

C: I think so.

T: Imagine this is a good place, where there is no pain. It's a safe and protected place.

C: OK.

T: So, whenever you need to, if the pain becomes too great, you can always come to this place where there is no pain. Ok? Good. Now step back to where you were before. You are Grace's Pain. Tell me a little about yourself.

C: I'm a very strong pain that starts here in her back... When I get it, I can't even think. I don't even want anyone to talk to me. My head also hurts a lot. Sometimes I just can't stand it. And the weirdest thing is that sometimes the pain in one finger or another finger of my hands. And sometimes the pain goes to my feet. And other times it comes up. It just seems to grab me and wrap me up, like it was stuck on me. I want to get rid of it and I can't.

T: When you think about that situation...you had said to me that you feel like you're trapped. When you think about the pain and the words, "I'm trapped", what comes up for you?

C: Yes, I'm trapped with this pain.

T: So far, you have been speaking as Grace with her pain. Now I want you to take one more step and be Grace's pain, OK?

Pain. Grace's Pain. I want you to stand here. (She moves over a step on the stage.) This is where Pain is. And this is Grace with her pain and over there is the place where there's no pain. Ok? (The therapist points out those places onstage.)

Now you are Grace's Pain. Tell me, how long have you been here? When did you come into Grace's life?

C: I don't remember.

T: Think about it a little bit. Were you with her when she was going to school?

C: No. I think she was like seven years old.

T: Grace was seven?

C: Grace was seven when I came into her life. Yes, it was then the headaches began, the pain in her head.

T: What happened to Grace at age seven that allowed you to come in?

C: Grace was a little girl that nobody liked. She had physical defects, learning disabilities; a middle child that no one wanted. She was abused, and yet couldn't say anything about it.

T: So when she was seven years old, you were already there. Was this something that went on for a long time or was it a one-time experience?

C: Until she was 15.

T: A lot of years. And Grace knew who was abusing her?

C: Yes.

T: Do you feel that you can tell us?

C: Yes, it was her brother.

T: And Grace tried to talk with her parents about it?

C: She didn't dare, because she felt threatened.

T: What was said to her?

C: That no one would believe her. That they would put the blame on her. That he would kill her if she told anyone; those kinds of things... threats.

T: You are Grace's Pain. How do you feel here as Grace's pain?

C: That I'm very strong. That I'm stronger than her. Sometimes I think I can dominate her.

T: Ok. What kinds of things do you say to Grace?

C: I make her suffer. I make her cry. I make her go through the same thing over and over again. And I don't want to go away. I don't want to leave her.

T: So you want to stay with her. How come?

C: Because I've become part of her now. We already have a relationship, an affection of sorts.

T: You are part of the folks that live inside her now.

C: Yes.

T: You know, Yolanda told me that Grace drew a picture of you. Do you remember that?

C: Yes.

T: Tell me what it looked like.

C: It was a red ball, with a lot black spots and lots of scratches. But she also drew a body, like a doll. She painted me there, very black and stuck to her.

T: When you think about these drawings, what do you think about yourself, Pain? What do you feel here? As Pain.

C: I think that somehow I got myself in here and that the drawing doesn't represent it all. I'm stronger.

T: You're stronger... Ok. And when you think of this drawing, what do you think about yourself that is negative and irrational?

C: I don't know. I am black. That's why I turn red. I don't know. I'm just stronger than she is.

T: So, you are a pain with all these characteristics. And your job is to hurt Grace. You're strong and ugly. You said something about being ugly. Can we say "I'm ugly"?

C: Yes, I'm ugly.

T: I want to take two steps in this direction, to that place where there is no pain. [Grace's Pain takes a few steps over onstage.) When you think, there's no pain here, I'm fine what are the positive things you think about yourself?

C: I think that maybe there are moments when I can get rid of this thing that's stuck to me and rip it off me, take it off, put it aside, and feel like I can move again. Because the pain paralyzes me. That's what I think that somehow... I see a white light... This white light makes me believe that I can heal.

T: So, what do you think of the phrase, "I can heal"?

C: It sounds good.

T: Ok. On a scale of one to seven, where seven is completely true and one is completely false, how true do you feel these words are now?

C: Three or four.

T: Ok. Go back to being the Pain. [She takes a few steps back to where she was before.] You said, "I am ugly. And when you think of these experiences, this pain... all that has happened to Grace... what emotions come up for you?

C: Anger. A lot of anger. I want to pick a fight with the whole world.

T: From zero to ten, where ten is the maximum disturbance and zero is none, how much does it bother you now when you think about that?

C: Ten.

T: And where do you feel it in your body?

C: Here. Back here, on my back. And sometimes it hurts a lot. It just grabs me.

T: So, you already know how EMDR works... I'll do a few eye movements. You can always ask me to stop if you want. Let's see what happens to you, Pain. As we do some processing, tell me what's happening to you.

So, think about what Grace went through... Think about the function of Grace's pain. Think about the words "I'm ugly." Feel that in your body. And follow my movements. (BLS)

T: Take a deep breath.

C: It's as if there were something here... I feel like crying. I want to remove it.

T: Let's go with that. (BLS)

T: And now?

C: I feel a lot of anger.

T: Can we keep going? (BLS)

T: Take a deep breath.

C: I think maybe I'm not that ugly. (BLS)

T: Take a deep breath

C: Once, Grace cut me off, pulled me out, she let me on the floor, she left me somewhere and I felt weird, as I do in this place. I have always been attached to her.

T: When you're not attached to her, what are you doing?

C: I don't leave her alone. I make her suffer.

T: And you follow her around?

C: Always.

T: So that she's not alone?

C: The truth is that we have been together for so long...

T: She can't imagine her life without you.

C: No.

T: It seems that the company has been painful but it's still company.

C: Yes.

T: I have a feeling, sometimes I'm wrong, but I have a feeling that somehow you also help her.

C: Maybe.

T: How do you think that happens?

C: I think that when she's in pain she also feels alive. Because sometimes she feels like she's dead, like she doesn't exist. I also give her a lot of attention. A lot.

T: And you help her to be quiet so that no one knows what happened with the threats. Somehow you protect her. Right?

C: Yes.

T: So you follow her around, you make her see she's alive; that she's not dead. You make her see that she can feel. And you protect her. Those seem like very important roles. So I'm not surprised that when she tries to get rid of you, you come back.

C: I hadn't thought about it like that before, but it makes sense.

T: Think about it. (BLS)

C: I thought about what I could do to help her. Because I had never thought about it that way... that I could get away from her...

T: I think it's important that you maintain your helper role. It seems that you have an important role, which is to denounce what was done to her: you say, "Look... I was abused, mistreated, people did things to me... I was threatened, they didn't let me talk..." And you are the spokesperson for all this. You are her pain. "Look, I exist. People did things to me and her mother doesn't acknowledge, and neither does her father or her brother". Someone has to recognize it.

C: Is that why I accompany her?

T: Think about it. (BLS)

C: I feel better now, calmer.

T: What happened?

C: I'm here for a reason.

T: That's right. I'm going to give you my opinion. I'm not always right, ok? I make mistakes, so you're the one who knows, who's right. But I'm going to give you my hunch anyway. Let's see what you think. The impression I have is that you, as Pain, need to be acknowledged. The only way you can change, turn into something else, and stop hurting so much is if somebody important acknowledges you. Recognizes what you went through, the pain, and what they did to her. What do you think?

C: I like that.

T: So, I have a suggestion. There are a lot of people here really anxious to recognize Grace's pain. How about we give them a chance, and give you, as Pain, an opportunity to be acknowledged? When that happens, sometimes it is possible to change the perception. (It's something magical, a chemical substance that our brain produces). And instead of Pain, maybe you could become Acknowledgement?

C: I would like to try that.

T: So, let's do the following: I want you to look around at all the people who are here. [Therapist turns Grace's Pain around so that she can see everyone in the audience. There is a mortal silence in the room. Everyone is looking at her and recognizing what she went through.] Everyone here is acknowledging Grace's Pain. Me too. I'm also acknowledging it. I see you. I see what Grace went through. It's not right that a young girl suffered so much in silence, for so many years without anyone to help her, to acknowledge what was happening to her. She had no one to say to her, "Yes, it's true what is happening to you. It's true. It's awful, and it's really happening." (BLS)

T: And now...?

C: Now I don't know very well what I have to do. I need help to figure out what I'm going to do if I continue being part of her life, if I help her... I'm a little confused.

T: Yes, that's normal. I'll tell you a few things and you tell me what you think. I remember that I read once that the problem of trauma - and Grace is very traumatized. The problem with trauma is that one has to try to digest the truth; the truth about what really happened. Grace really suffered all those things. And you are the one who has been denouncing it and recognizing it, wanting that this pain be acknowledged. I also learned that perception is everything. You are Grace's perception and you have an important role to play in her life; a role of protection, help, company, or acknowledgement of the truth. So, it's not just a matter of throwing it away... that's why it comes back.

C: I want to tell Grace that it is over, but I don't know how. I want to say that I recognize that she suffers and that I know why she suffers, how much she has suffered, how much pain she has. But I don't know, as Pain, how to tell her that.

T: What ways do we have to communicate?

C: We have verbal communication... or what happens when she endures the pain. When she says, "It hurts here"... When she draws me, the pain, that's communication.

T: You know Grace well... what do you think is the best way to communicate this information to her? In a way that she can believe that this can come in and do her good?

C: I know she's very spiritual and she prefers to communicate with a spiritual entity than with someone who exists. She believes a lot in protectors and angels.

T: So, she has other companions. There are more folks inside her Inner Gallery. So, can you imagine yourself communicating with Grace directly, or do you want do it through her angels?

C: I think I want to communicate with her angels, because direct communication hasn't been good.

T: I want you to give this information to Grace's angels. (BLS)

C: It was hard to communicate with this angel... but I recognized it by its light.

T: So, the message has been sent. Ok. When we started, you were Grace's Pain. And we saw that you have important roles of protection, support, and acknowledgement of what she has gone through. Who are you now?

C: I'm not really sure, but it's someone inside her Inner Gallery.

T: If you had to say positive words about yourself, and if you could transform the pain into something else, what would that be?

C: I'd like to be a white light of healing.

T: OK. And if you become this white light of healing what are the positive words that go with that?

C: I'm going to help you to overcome all these things that have happened to you; to acknowledge the pain and feel better.

T: Ok. So, how does "I can help you" sound? Instead of pain, how about believing the words, I can help you, and on a scale of one to seven, where seven is completely true and one is completely false, how true do you feel these words are for you now?

C: Seven. (BLS)

T: Powerful seven?

C: Powerful seven!

T: I want to thank you for having come here today and taught us so much. Thank you for the opportunity we had to acknowledge you and give Grace this opportunity to be healed a bit more. Now, I'm going to ask you to go back to being Grace with Pain. Now she needs to hear all of this information that you have discovered, OK?

T: Take a step over here, please. [The therapist now begins talking to this new role onstage.]

Grace with Pain, I've just had a long conversation with your Pain and she told me a lot of interesting things. She passed on some information to one of your angels. So, I would like for you to listen to what this angel has to tell you, Ok? (BLS)

T: How are you now?

C: I'm good. I didn't know that you [the angel] could help me. I always knew that you could help me, but it never occurred to me to ask for help.

T: And now?

C: I know it's going to help me. The role isn't just to protect me, but to help me overcome everything I have been through in life; to be able to get out of this mess, because I can't take this anymore. (BLS)

T: How are you now?

C: I'm calmer, because now I know that I have a different way to look at this, not so ugly, or morbid. Now I know that there is something I can do to get better.

T: When you think of the words "there's something I can do"... From one to seven, seven being completely true, and one being completely false, how true do you feel these words are now?

C: Like... six.

T: Think about it. (BLS)

T: And now?

C: I feel there is something I want to get out of here, but I don't know what it is. [She puts her hand on her chest.] It's something that tightens my chest and hurts a lot, but that needs to come out. There are so many things I need to say but I can't. (BLS)

T: That's OK, you don't have to tell us, just think about it. (BLS)

C: It's very important for me to talk, because I've never had someone who would listen to me. So I need to tell you. All my life, I have kept this secret. All my life, I've been rejected. All my life, I've been a person who didn't really exist. Sometimes, my body paralyzes. And that's when the pain would get at me harder. When I felt paralyzed. And today, for the first time in a long time there was a light of hope at the end of the tunnel for me.

T: Think about that. (BLS)

T: And now?

C: I felt that there was a knot here in the middle, and it started to come out, little by little; something that bothered me, as if it wanted to come out on its own. I felt some relief when it came out.

T: Grace, you've had a lot of pain for a lot of years. And it must have hurt intensely. Tell me if you believe that this can all come out now, or if this is going to be a process that will need to be accompanied?

C: It's a process that will accompany me.

T: Ok. So, we are going to help you so that this process can move forward. You told me that now you believe that you have help and that this pain can be healed. How about we place aside this part of the pain that needs to continue to heal and that will be treated by Yolanda? I think she will better understand how to help you now. Let's leave it aside for now, put it in a little box…? And let's work a little on the tools that you have, these resources, these new words, this new understanding of your pain, and the acknowledgement of your pain. What do you think?

C: I like it. (BLS)

T: Ok. So, how are you now?

C: I'm better, much better.

T: So, I'd like to give you a little taste of what your life will be like in the future. Take a step over here. Do you remember we had talked about the Grace with No Pain? I want you to feel for a moment how Grace will be in the future, the one that you will be able to live without pain; because the pain is past now, over with. Since it was acknowledged, it can now dissolve, metabolize and come to a good resolution eventually.

C: I really want to live that.

T: And here, in this place, you can live without pain. [Steps over to the place the therapist points out to her onstage.] How do you feel here?

C: I feel like a weight was taken off of me, because it weighed me down. I was wrapped up in it, and now I feel like I can move around.

T: You had said, "I can move around" and you also said, "I can heal". Which one connects with you more?

C: I can be healed. I can be healed.

T: And on a scale of one to seven... Seven being completely true, and one being completely false, how true do you feel these words are for you now?

C: Seven. Seven.

T: So, I want you to think about these words that represent your future, and follow my fingers. (BLS)

T: And now?

C: Now I feel that I want to continue. I want to have more therapy sessions, and have more opportunities to do this kind of reprocessing. It has become really important for me. I need to heal, and I have to do it in baby steps, little by little.

T: Grace, I want to thank you once again for coming here; for sharing your pain with us, and for giving us the opportunity to acknowledge your pain, this pain has helped you and that starts to be transformed. It will take on other forms in your life. And now you have this future full of hope that includes, "I can heal". I want thank you very much for sharing all this with us. Now, I'd like to ask you to change back to being Yolanda. Take a step over here. [Takes a few steps sideways.]

What have you learned, Yolanda?

C: I learned something that had never occurred to me before: that the pain could be part of her Inner Gallery; perhaps the most absolute entity of these folks inside. And I learned that I feel. Because many times we say we understand people, in theory, but now that I was Grace, *I felt what she felt*... it's different.

T: How do you feel now when you think of going back to your office and seeing Grace again?

C: I feel much better about it. This has helped give me a new perspective about how I can help her. I brought her case here because I really didn't know where to go with it anymore. Now I see that I need to process her pain as well and not just her trauma. I had thought about going back to her childhood, and treating those experiences, but not in this wonderful way. I'm very grateful for this technique. It had never occurred to me, because a lot of people come to me with pain, but I had not understood that this was a part their Inner Gallery. Even pain is a role, as if it were a kind of personality. It has a function, a reason to exist, a story, a discourse.

T: Yes, and that's why it is possible to treat it, too.

C: I'm very grateful for having been able to present this very difficult case, and for your helping me as a therapist, as a psychologist, to help my patient.

T: That's why it's important that we have these tools, because many times we also learn from our patients what it is that we need to do, what decision we need to make. So I thank you from the bottom of my heart for having shared all of this with us.

My thoughts and comments at the end of this session:
Different roles came up. I work a lot with the metaphor, the symbol, because they have a greater power of generalization. I suspected from the very beginning when I heard Yolanda's case, that this was an issue of pain. I thought, *if we don't treat this pain, nothing else is going to move here.* We had to unblock this stuff. Sometimes it's not a matter of a concrete situation, but all of her pain. So, I took this shortcut, and went straight for her pain, so that we could understand what function the pain was fulfilling in her life. It was something that even she herself did not understand.

Here it was not a matter of expelling someone who lived inside, because it would have come back. If one does not care properly for the roles, they do come back. That's why symptoms come back. You have to find out what the symptom is denouncing; what it is that needs to heal. Symptoms tell us that something is not well... It's like a fever that tells us that there is an infection. If you don't heal the cause of this infection, the person doesn't heal.

So, since I didn't know what the cause was I tried to create a situation where the patient (and her blessed brain) could find their way. Sometimes, we need to give information; sometimes we need to re-structure the situation in such a way that they can understand what is going on. We can suggest something and if this makes sense to the patient, they will accept it. But when they say, "No, it's not like that" it's also helpful. I have no problem when a patient says "no" to me because it gives me the opportunity to ask, "Then, what is it?" After all, I am at the service of this client, and not to my self-esteem issues. I want to give them the best I have in terms of tools so that the person can find the structure that will bring about healing.

Now, this is a case, as all of you realized, where there is immense pain. It's not a pain that can be resolved in one session. I wanted to help this patient (in truth, this therapist) to take one more step forward in her healing process. I think we were able to see that "Grace" was able to open this small hole through which the pain could begin to come out. And through which it was able to transform itself, once it was recognized and acknowledged.

I believe that one of the biggest problems with pain has to do with the lack of acknowledgement. Nobody believed that this had happened to Grace. Many patients get to the point where they think: I'm imagining all of this; it's a lie. And if someone doesn't recognize and acknowledge my pain, it's like, I'm invisible. I don't exist. And that can be a good (and unfortunate) proposal for suicide.

I took advantage of the opportunity that all of us could become part of Grace's Inner Gallery, because she needed this level of recognition of her pain. I asked for your help, from the audience, because I wasn't sure that just my own acknowledgement would have been enough because her pain was so great. So when she received a lot of acknowledgment she was able to transform this into the kind of help she needed. She was able to find her way.

I tried to identify the roles so that they became clear to her. But it was at the ending, when she was able to see Grace's future without pain, that hope finally became a reality for her.

She needed a lot of people in her Inner Gallery. She didn't have her husband's support. And you folks here today were so loving, and compassionate. I felt such an attunement with all of you even though there were so many of you. [There were more than 150 people present at this workshop.] So I ran the risk of including you because I felt that she needed *a lot* of acknowledgment. She was abused from ages seven to fifteen. By the time she was fifteen, half of her life had been sheer abuse. Her mother or father never acknowledged it. And that is why I did something big here today.

Final comments:

As I was re-reading this after several years, I thought it was important to add a few more comments about how this session was conducted.

I didn't work directly with Grace's abuse because I suspected dissociation. When we encounter a patient with a long history of sexual abuse/incest over a long period of time in childhood, chances are we are facing a situation of probable dissociation. That is why I didn't go straight for the traumas.

Since Yolanda had mentioned that she didn't have a lot of time to treat Grace before she moved away, I thought it would be better to offer Yolanda a map that would guide her during the little time they had left. I didn't believe it would have been prudent to open up the box of abuse for the same reason: there just wasn't going to be enough time to work through that without a high risk of the client dissociating.

Healing the pain first was one way of treating the problem in a fragile patient. It gave Grace more resources. With the emotional distance we gave her, she was better able to see the role of pain in her life and find a solution. Although the issue of pain was not totally resolved – nor would that have been a reasonable expectation for one session – at least the function of the pain began to make sense to Grace. It gave her a way out.

Treating the pain was also a shortcut. Can you imagine how many abuse scenes would have to be worked through? And how many sessions that would take? Working through the pain allowed us the possibility of generalizing the relief to other neuronetworks.

At the end of the session I asked Grace to role-reverse with the role of Grace Without Pain. That served two purposes. First, it allowed Grace to end the session in a resource place. We had created this role as a Safe Place, where she could go if she couldn't stand the pain. But it also served as a future goal, and gave her the hope that this could become something she could reach at some point in her life. That way the session ended on a strong note, full of possibilities. A traumatized child has no sense of future. When we were able to take Grace's Inner Child to a place where she could believe that a future without pain was possible, we knew we were on the right track.

Finally, working with the Inner Gallery is a way to avoid dissociation during reprocessing. If we let the work go on internally we don't always know what is happening inside the person. The patient may dissociate and the therapist doesn't perceive it. If we place the roles on the outside – on a stage as do Psychodramatists, or use the Inner Gallery Kit[23], or with the *Play of Life Kit*[24] as is taught in courses of role theory – the patient will create a greater emotional distance, and can maintain the dual attention necessary for the reprocessing to continue at a rate the client can deal with well.

---

[23] A small box of ceramic pieces and a micro-stage used to map out the Inner Gallery of Roles that therapists can be trained quickly to use in lieu of Psychodrama. See the author's book, _Healing the Folks Who Live Inside_ for an example, or contact the author for training opportunities. See www.plazacounselingservices.com

[24] Developed by Carlos Raimundo, MD, Australian psychiatrist and psychodramatist, who developed a form of mapping out roles with the use of Playmobil®. See, www.playoflife.com

Medical Interventions

Amputation and Phantom Limb Pain

In historical terms, we know that during the US Civil War during the decade of 1860, produced a wave of soldier amputees that complained of pain in their amputated limbs[25]. Some attributed it to some "phantom" or "ghost", or perhaps a hallucination, which led to the terms *causalgia* or phantom member. Nowadays, it is estimated that a feeling or pain in the phantom limb is present in the majority of people who undergo amputation (between 50-90%, depending on the study [Desmond & MacLachlan, 2002; Sherman, Sherman, & Parker, 1984[26]]) with a chronic incidence that varies between 10-78% (Beckham et al., 1997; Sherman et al., 1984[27]). Since it is frequently conjugated with Post-Traumatic Stress Disorder (PTSD), many patients also develop depression as a result of the disease that led to the amputation or with regard to the amputation itself.

A recent study (Poundja et al.,2006), with 130 US veterans showed a high correlation (89.5%) between PTSD and the severity of the pain, with depression. This suggests the importance of interventions that will effectively treat both PTSD and depression as well as the chronic pain, like phantom limb pain.

A colleague, Glaci Faingluz, who treated a patient who had undergone a recent amputation a few days before this session, wrote up the following narrative. Glaci was touched by this person's suffering and saw her while she was still in the hospital, recovering from the operation that severed her leg. It has been seen that EMDR therapy is one of the few tools

---

[25] Russell, M. C. (2008). Treating Traumatic Amputation-Related Phantom Limb Pain: A Case Study Utilizing Eye Movement Desensitization and Reprocessing Within the Armed Services, *Clinical Case Studies*, 7 (2) 136-153.

[26] Desmond, D., & MacLachlan, M. (2002). Psychosocial issues in the field of prosthetics and orthotics. *Journal of Prosthetics and Orthotics*, 14(2), 19.
Sherman, R. A., Sherman, C. J., & Parker, L. (1984). Chronic phantom and stump pain among American veterans: Results of a survey. *Pain, 18*(1), 83-95.

[27] Beckham, J. C., Crawford, A. L., Feldman, M. E., Kirby, A. C., Hertzberg, M. A., Davidson, J. R. T., et al. (1997). Chronic posttraumatic stress disorder and chronic pain in Vietnam combat veterans. *Journal of Psychosomatic Research*, 43(4), 379-389.
Sherman, R. A., Sherman, C. J., & Parker, L. (1984). Chronic phantom and stump pain among American veterans: Results of a survey. *Pain, 18*(1), 83-95.

available that decreases or eliminates phantom limb pain[28]. See how Manuela was able to overcome the physical pain as a result of this session.

Manuela was 57 years old when it became necessary to amputate her leg due to blood circulation problems. The EMDR therapist, Glaci, had seen the patient on several occasions at the hospital. Touched by how much pain Manuela still felt in her phantom limb, she proposed an EMDR session in order to ease her suffering. Manuela really wanted the pain to stop and no one seemed to know what to do to help her. The doctors had increased her medication, but even so, the pain didn't go away. Manuela couldn't understand how she could feel so much pain in a member she no longer had. It is important to underline that she was receiving a high dosage of medication before the EMDR session, but that even so, the pain persisted.

She set up the classic protocol, using the amputated leg as the image, a negative cognition about the pain in her leg, the emotions of sadness (SUDS = 8 for the experience of the amputation), with sensations in her (amputated) foot. The desired positive cognition was that she could live as an amputee but without pain. [Tactile bilateral movements were used in this case.]

When the client thought about her situation, she still saw herself with her leg. She remembered the sadness and discomfort with the surgery itself, and felt an itching in her missing foot. The measure on the pain scale went up at this point.

As the reprocessing continued she was able to see her stump without the leg. This made her even sadder. Suddenly, it occurred to her to say goodbye to her amputated leg:

"So I spoke with my leg and said that I was going to miss it. We were born together, grew up together. But the sad moment had come when I would have to learn to live without it so that I could move on with my life". The reprocessing continued while the client said goodbye to her leg, in touch with this sense of loss. Finally, the client opened her eyes, and said, *"I said goodbye to the leg. The stump told me everything is going to be OK, that I will have my difficulties, but that I am going to be able to adapt."*

Now when the therapist asked how much it bothered her to have lost her leg she said zero. It didn't bother her anymore. She still felt a tingling in her leg, with a SUDS of four (on a scale of zero to ten). They reprocessed that feeling until she no longer felt any more physical pain.

---

[28] Meignant, I. (2012, October). [The treatment of limb pain phantom EMDR]. *Annals of Physical and Rehabilitation Medicine*, 55(Supplement 1), e85-e86. doi:10.1016/j.rehab.2012.07.214. French

They discussed how the client would incorporate this new identity. It would probably happen a little bit at a time. The session lasted about 50 minutes and the therapist ended the session with a relaxation exercise, finalizing by having her go to her Calm Place that had been installed earlier.

The following day, the amount of meds was reduced by half, and on the third day after this session, she no longer took any pain medication at all. The client was able to continue her recovery in a much better mood since she no longer had any phantom limb pain at all. That also allowed her to do better with physiotherapy. She was more motivated and focused after having "said goodbye to her leg".

Glaci comments: *There was a "domino effect", that is, a general improvement overall for the patient, after having treated a specific and traumatic event (in this case, the amputation of her leg.) Something real is happening. We have the gratifying feeling of helping someone with their pain. And the certainty of having contributed not only to reduce this person's pain, but the expectation of reducing pain that is present in the lives of so many others, including ourselves. The possibility of "amputating" the pain of life that people have, using EMDR therapy brings new perspective for treatment, for both acute pain as well as chronic. This encourages us to continue with our work to improve the quality of life of those we treat.*

Four months later, at follow-up, Manuela reported that she had had no pain in her phantom limb since the day of the EMDR session.

Miranda and knee surgery

Miranda, was 57 years old when she arrived at the clinic, extremely anxious because of a recent knee surgery. It had turned her life upside down. Here's the story in her own words:

"I had knee surgery about a month ago. Ah! Just talking about it makes me cry! Many things that happened during the surgery traumatized me. I've had some problems for six months now... I had to do an MRI for the knee and I could not go into the tube. It was awful to have to do that. I wound up doing it under sedation, but only after I had procrastinated as much as I could. Even so, I was deathly afraid. The closed room, the building had an elevator that I had to go up in order to do the MRI.

"There was a time in my life that I was well balanced, so much so that I didn't have these issues of fear, anxiety, heart palpitations. It was a good phase. I lived like that for a long time. But I don't know if it was the result of the trauma with my knee, I began to sleep poorly.

"I had already had several medical interventions on my knee, tendons, meniscus. My knee was really in a bad way. I never had a fall; it was just the result of being overweight. I went to do the tests (I did these MRIs with sedation as well), but when I got to the hospital, and I had to go in…! I spoke with the anesthesiologist and asked him not to close the door… I told him I couldn't go into the tube if I was awake. I did the test and went home. I wasn't so afraid. I was able to do the exam. The result of it was that I had to go to surgery.

"I set the date for the operation. I was really anxious. I wasn't afraid of the surgery itself, but of the surgical center. It's hard to be in there. I explained to the anesthesiologist again that I had a phobia about being in closed spaces, lying down. It's one of those places where you can't even raise your head. I would think about that and get anxious. I asked him to do the anesthesia as fast as possible so I could go back to my hospital room quickly. The surgery was to last 40 minutes, and there I went, straight into a tiny prep room. No window! Where's the door? I got really anxious.

"They took me to the operating room, and when I got there, they called me by another name! I told them my name. I called the nurse and told her I couldn't be alone. I felt so alone! People would come in and out. On top of that, they made a mistake with my name! I was so afraid and anxious. I had had other surgeries before, but nothing like this. I have a real phobia about being in a closed room! No one would calm me down.

"Finally, the anesthesiologist arrived. I went to sleep. When I woke up the surgery was over. I spent three hours in the recovery room, looking at the ceiling. Other people in there were snoring; there was all this machinery. No one stayed with me. I kept saying I wanted to go to my hospital room. It was three hours of pure agony. I prayed. I sang.

"I've had other surgeries before, but this one was different. When I finally got to my room, I was tense and anxious. My leg really hurt. It was really painful. I wanted to know about the meds they were giving me. They gave me something and turned out the light, and told me I would go to sleep. I asked them to turn the light on again. I was afraid of being alone. I decided to read the explanation about what meds I was taking, and as a result, didn't want to take it anymore. The nurse stopped giving me one of them. I stopped taking two of the pills because I read what they could do to me. I couldn't breathe. I went to the window for some air. I told them, "I'm not feeling well." Ever since that day, I can't stand to be by myself. I'm afraid I'll get sick or something and have to go back to the hospital.

"I went to the cardiologist. He says I'm fine. No problems with my heart, normal blood pressure, heartbeat. I felt like my heart was beating too fast. He gave me some natural medication. I took it and felt better. I was still afraid for a few days, but the fear began to get better. I was getting it under control. When a friend of mine came to visit, I was still dealing with these fears. Now it has been a month since the surgery, and I've been better in the last two weeks. I can even sleep at night. I have never been afraid of being alone. Now I have to have someone with me all the time.

"My fear is so great that I wanted to make an appointment with another therapist who worked in a place without an elevator, like you have here in your building. Where I do physiotherapy I can manage to get into the elevator now, while my husband parks the car. That was progress."

After the usual preparation for EMDR therapy, we began reprocessing the recent experience and her issues with the surgery. We began with the scene of the operation, when the client mentioned she felt she was going to suffocate, and shared her emotions of anxiety and fear. Miranda wanted to go back to being the brave person she had always been, able to face her circumstances in a functional manner, but she just couldn't see how to do that. Her fear and anxiety were a five on the SUDS scale of zero to ten. She said, "I still want to cry, but it's gotten better." She said she felt these things in her chest and mouth.

I asked her to look at her experiences with the surgery as if it were like a video, since this was a recent event in her life. Not enough time had gone by for it to consolidate into more concrete memory. Miranda commented that the video began when she went into the operating room. After the initial movements to get the speed right, we did a long set of bilateral movements, about 200, on a light bar. When we stopped, Miranda said:

"I was able to think about all of that, and what I'm like after the surgery. Now I have the feeling that it is over. It was a moment that I had to go through, but it's over. I was able to remember everything, the scenes, the anguish of having to lie down. It was just a moment. But when I do this exercise, I still feel the sensation in my tummy, in my stomach."

The therapist continued with the bilateral movements.

C: What was really tight has calmed down now.

T: And now, when you think about that difficult experience, on a scale of zero to ten, where ten is the worst disturbance you can imagine, and zero is nothing, how much does it bother you now?

C: Right now I have no more fear. I don't feel fear when I think about it. I have the feeling that it was something that happened, and it's over, and the consequences are also going to go away. I don't want to have the fear of being alone anymore. I want to go back to being that courageous person that I've always been and that in some moments I have been able to recover. I don't feel like crying anymore. It's like I'm searching for something in other people.

The therapist ended the session explain how the reprocessing often continues after the session, and they set the appointment for the following week.

At the next appointment, Miranda said:

"I am really a lot better. I'm able to walk better with my knee. There are some things that still bother me: I'm afraid of the hospital, of doctors, of medicine. When I think I may have to go back to the hospital, I get a bad feeling in the pit of my stomach. It's so bad I made an appointment with the doctor. It's really bad. It bothers me here (and points to her stomach). This fear…it's been terrifying. I was never afraid of anything the way I have been lately. I'm still not free of this giant in my life. I used to be able to listen to all of the bad news on TV, but now I can't.

The therapist asked her to think about what they had worked on in the last session, and if anything had changed. Miranda answered:

C: It's not the same. It still bothers me a little bit, more than a zero, like a 3 or 4. When I think about how lonely I felt, and that I had to stay lying down in that position! All that time… without anyone nearby. In that closed up place. I still remember that. "The therapist set things up to continue reprocessing and they did another long set.

C: Now I was able to remember these difficult things in a calmer fashion, with more serenity, and not all that despair. I don't have that bad feeling in the pit of my stomach. Before, I just couldn't stand it, but I can still feel it now (and points to her body).

T: Put your hand on your body on the place where you still feel that and look at the light bar. (BLS)

C: Now I feel relief in my stomach. It's really different. I want to go back to my point of equilibrium.

C: I had an interesting experience this last week. A little girl died, who was like a niece to me. She had leukemia. The transplanted medulla had taken, but even so, she died. I thought, how am I am going to face that without falling apart? But you know what? I was able to take the news calmly. We had enormous affection for her, but we didn't despair. I felt a good balance, a good equilibrium in that situation.

I thought: *Will my fears come back now that I've heard she's passed away?* But, no, they didn't. I wasn't afraid. My husband went out, and I was by myself in the house. This was new. I didn't have to go to my son's house like I've had to do since the surgery. I was able to stay at home without anguish. I thought this was very, very good. I'm beginning to feel stronger that way. After the surgery I had a hard time even being in my bedroom. Everything bothered me. I would go outside and sit on a bench. I had these accusing thoughts. I love my home. I wasn't like this before. Now I'm getting over it. Sometimes I get a little something, but it's not like it was, no way!

T: And now, how much does it bother you?

C: It's OK. I'm not going to say it's a zero. It's about a two. It still bothers me. But look, I was able to go up the elevator in your building today, all by myself! And I sat in the waiting room all by myself. Before, I wasn't able to do that. And I didn't have any bad feelings. Right now, I feel much lighter. (BLS)

C: I'm getting calmer.

C: I'm also sleeping better. I'm eating normally. I'm doing things more freely. Very nice, this improvement.

T: (Checking some of her triggers.) Let's think about when you have to return to the hospital?

C: Not a problem. When I went back to take the stitches out, I wasn't able to go into the hospital. I kept going back to the door. That was eight days after the surgery. When I finally went in, I stayed in the waiting room I couldn't stand to be there. Now when I think about it, it's ok. As a matter of fact, I am going there when I leave your office.

T: Then think about going there and let's see if you can do it. (BLS)

C: It's fine. You know, my husband is going to travel on Friday, and I'm good about it. I think that if it had been like it was before, I wouldn't have been able to stay alone while he was traveling.

The therapist ended the session, and they set up the next appointment.

When the therapist asked Miranda how she was doing at the following session, she replied:

C: I'm fine. I went to the doctor and it went well. I came up the elevator here in your building just now. I was sitting by myself in your waiting room. The terror is gone.

C: Yesterday, my daughter got sick and had to go to the hospital. I went with her. The part where they give out the meds is way inside. Well, I was able to go with her. I stayed the whole time. No panic. I thought, wow, am I going to be able to stay in there with her? Am I going to have to ask my husband to help her? But, no. I stayed there whole time. I walked around there by myself, without fear. Sometimes I thought, am I going to freak out? Or are those feelings going to come back? But I'm able to do everything without fear. Before, I couldn't get near the hospital door!

C: My husband went on his trip on Friday, and I stayed home alone. I took the car. It is an automatic transmission and I can drive with the other leg. I just went down the street to get some money out of the bank. I went in. I left. I went to the supermarket, and picked up what I needed. I went home... no worries. I drove by myself and felt fine. Later I went to physiotherapy, all by myself. Before, I would go there and keep looking out for my husband, very dependent on his presence. But not anymore. Sometimes I wonder if I'm going to have a problem.

C: The day before he traveled, my husband said to me that I should go home in a taxi after our session. I had read somewhere about people getting kidnapped in taxies, and I was scared. Wow, what if it wasn't a real taxi driver? But I had the courage to get in the taxi and go home. I wasn't scared or afraid. All of these things I've been able to do without freaking out. I can stay home till 7 p.m. when my son gets there. So, I only have good things to tell you. I'm finding my balance.

C: I see that I lack one little thing. Sometimes I feel insecure, but I don't know what it is. I work at it and I'm able to overcome it, but I still have this little bit of insecurity.

C: I have this thing inside that scares me. Sometimes I hear, oh, so-and-so really lost his mind. I've never seen somebody who really did that, lose their mind. And I thought, I wonder if that's what's happening to me? Am I losing my mind? But now I don't think about that anymore. But I still have a little fear that maybe I could lose my mind.

The therapist set up the processing protocol, targeting this insecurity that Miranda described.

C: I think I could lose my mind and go crazy; that I'm imbalanced. That I would have to take those horrible meds and I have a real reluctance to taking medication. I panic just thinking about it.

T: And when you think about this insecurity, and these negative words, this feeling of panic, how much does it bother you?

C: About an eight.

T: And where do you feel it in your body?

C: The pit of my stomach.

The therapist asks Miranda to think about all of these things and look at the light bar. (BLS)

C: I thought about it, but I didn't get upset. I thought about what could happen, and it didn't bother me.

T: So now, when you think about this difficult experience and the positive words, I am a balanced person, on a scale of one to seven, where seven is true and one is false, how true do you feel those words are?

C: Seven.

The therapist reinforces this good feeling with a few more bilateral movements, and the client says she doesn't feel any disturbance in her body.

C: It's very nice to think this way.

C: [To the therapist] I'm going to wait until my knee gets well and see if everything that I worked on here is going to turn out all right. I still feel bad that I can't do a lot of things I like because of my knee surgery. But I have to wait until my knee heals. I'm going to wait until all of this is over and see how I'm doing. Depending on how I am, I'll call again and make an appointment.

And that is how Miranda ended therapy.

Medicine and Antidotes

Rachel arrived to her session commenting on how scared she was. She had just left the doctor's office where he had insisted one more time that she needed to operate a benign tumor in her intestine that had been detected some time ago. Because of its location, it would be a delicate operation, and needed to be done with care. As a result she kept putting off. She had become very resistant to the idea of surgery.

"I left the doctor's office really scared. I thought, my body created this. I feel lost. And I need to face what I have."

We set up the EMDR protocol, and I asked her to draw how she perceived this tumor in her body.

Drawing #1

While she was looking at her picture, she said, *"There's something wrong with me. I would like to think that I am healthy. (VoC = 2), but I feel fear, sadness, in my chest and throat."*

We started the reprocessing:

Client (C): I have a Skeptic that lives inside of me that does not let me believe that I can get well. (BLS).

I deserve to go through this. (BLS) I think it has something to do with my mother, my grandmother, but it's kind of diffused. (BLS)

When I was born, my paternal grandmother didn't have any granddaughters, only grandsons. She hadn't accepted my parents' marriage. She didn't like my mother. She only came to accept her after I was born. I would spend extended periods at my grandmother's house with her, and my aunt. My mother didn't like it that I went, but there wasn't a lot she could do about it. I've worked on this before, with other therapists. I had a gastritis that was connected to my first separation from my mother. My grandmother always spoke ill of my mother, and I guess I sometimes I did, too. My grandmother was very rigid.

T: What is the punishment that we give a little girl for speaking ill of her mother?

C: A scene came to me. I was really mad at my mom. It was about something that I didn't like and she said that I couldn't treat my parents badly. (BLS)

I was very mad at the six-year-old little girl. She wasn't the way she was supposed to be. I had to do everything, obey, do well in school, and she didn't have to do any of this. (BLS)

She (the six-year-old) wants to punish me, but I don't let her exist the way she wants to. It is the opposite of how she wants to be (BLS).

T: How come she needs to be punished?

C: Because she has to fit in and she doesn't want to.

T: Why doesn't she want to?

C: Because she wants to be free.

T: And what keeps her from being free? (BLS)

C: She was told she has to fit in; she needs to think about others first.

T: Does that work?

C: No.

T: Then, go back there, and take care of this little girl, and take her out of that place that isn't hers. (BLS)

C: I picked her up and put her in my lap. The two of them are crying (BLS).

She says she doesn't want to hurt her, but she's afraid. I told her I would take care of her.

T: She's afraid of being punished because she wants to be free?

C: Afraid of not being able to be herself. I'm mad at myself because I don't let her be herself. (BLS)

I'm afraid of her. What would happen if I were like her?

T: What could happen?

C: People aren't going to like me anymore (BLS). I'm tired of being like this.

T: And you seem to be paying a high price for it, too…?

C: It's just that I have to fit the mold, and make sure people are OK.

T: Until when?

C: I don't want to do that anymore. (BLS)

I can learn with her, with this six-year-old girl. (BLS)

I'm the six-year-old! I'm afraid. She's not afraid. She's mad, and I can't be angry.

T: How come?

C: Because I feel guilty. (BLS)

She said that she thinks they can all go to hell. (BLS) I'm over 50, and I've spent my whole life pleasing others. Now it's time to please myself. (BLS)

I don't have to be afraid.

T: Either you please your grandmother or your mother – sounds pretty difficult. Do you think you can live as an adult, with your present age? (BLS)

C: I want to stop feeling guilty. Because if I do things one way, I feel guilty. If I do it another way, I feel guilty. There's no way out! I'm never going to be able to please everyone! (BLS)

I think that if I manage to please myself, that's plenty good. (BLS)

I want to recover the power over myself, over my body.

T: "I deserve to go through this." You said that earlier. Do you really deserve it?

C: No.

T: What have you got to say to your Skeptic then? The one you mentioned at the beginning of the session?

C: He still scares me. He's stronger than I am.

T: When you think about the six-year-old girl – what would you like to say to her?

C: That she can be herself. (BLS)

She doesn't have to please others. The important thing is for her to feel good about herself.

T: You, as an adult, can you afford to displease others in order to please yourself?

C: I still have this fear – of losing other people's love, people who are important to me. (BLS) (She changes physical posture.) Why, true love is unconditional! If I lost it, it's because it wasn't real to begin with!

T: So, you can run the risk?

C: I don't have to be perfect because nobody is perfect. And I can accept myself the way I am, in the same way that I accept others the way they are, or not, if I want to. (BLS)

T: So, you can choose the punishment, the punishment for the child, or you can let her run the risk of losing the conditional love of other people? Which do you want?

C: I want to be free. (BLS)

T: So, let's take this child out of time-out? End her punishment? How do we do that?

C: Let's pick her up and take her somewhere else. (BLS)

Something came to me right now. I do that, but I don't perceive it. The truth is that in practice, in truth, I am already doing the things I want to do. It's different from what I feel. I'm freer than I realize! (BLS)

Another part showed up, my young adult. A difficult moment, I'm afraid. Sometimes she takes the lead. She made bad choices. And paid for it.

T: She paid for it, but she doesn't need to keep on paying for it, does she?

C: That's right, she paid dearly for it. (BLS)

I told her that everything is all right. She doesn't need to be afraid.

T: So the little girl and the young adult are fitting together?

C: Yes. (BLS)

My body doesn't need to go through all of this either.

T: Then how about you say that to your body… that it doesn't deserve to go through all of this.

C: I call the shots here. Me! (BLS)

T: And what are you going to do with your Skeptic?

C: I am going to tell him to shut up and butt out! (BLS)

The Skeptic still scares me.

T: When we are six years old, the adults are much stronger than we are. (BLS)

C: But I'm not six anymore, haven't been for a long time. I can face the Skeptic… and tell him to shut up! (BLS)

I can make better choices.

T: Who are you going to feed? Everything we feed, grows. Whatever we don't feed, starves. Are you going to feed the Skeptic? The Adult? The Child? (BLS)

C: I opened the door and kicked him out the door! A good swift kick on his butt side (BLS)

T: And now, on a scale of zero to ten, how much does it bother you when you think about that first picture you drew?

C: Two. I'm still a bit afraid, a little bit. (BLS)

Remember the He-Man? And how he would say, "I have the Force!" Now it's a one of disturbance. Just a little teeny bit. (BLS)

I'm going to get to where I want to. (BLS)

OK, the SUDS is a one, I need to test myself a little bit.

T: You still have that thing in your intestine, right? Maybe that's why it can't get to zero?

C: Yeah, something like that.

T: Let's make another drawing? How you would like for it to be?

(See the following drawing.)

Drawing #2

C: [Client makes a new drawing] I am free, healthy and happy.

T: And when you think about this drawing and these positive words, I am free, healthy and happy, how much do you believe it is true now, on a scale of one to seven? Seven is completely true.

C: Six. (BLS) I'm on my way. I still lack... I need to know that this thing is going to go away or convince myself that it is going to be quiet.

T: What would be the medicine to heal this, now that you have the Force and no longer need to punish yourself? Before, the medicine wouldn't work. You had a Skeptic. You had a belief that you had to go through all of this, that you deserved it. We've broken the power of those things, so what would be your medicine?

C: My immune system... it's a like a band of piranhas that go there, eat it all up, and eliminate it. (BLS)

T: Let's strengthen that picture? (BLS)

C: I feel that the order had been given.

T: And this doctor for whom you have so much respect... how many times a day would he say you would have to take your medicine?

C: Three times a day for six months: in the morning, at lunch and at nighttime.

T: And what do you think about yourself when you ponder all of this?

C: I can heal myself. I have this picture of me taking my medicine. (BLS)

T: And on a scale of one to seven, now how true are these words, "I can heal myself"?

C: Seven. (BLS)

[Therapist strengthens this belief as the client thinks about drawing #2]. Another phrase came to me now: I can heal myself. I can do this treatment. (BLS)

And if I need help, I'm going to go after it.

T: So now, close our eyes, and scan your body, and think about these words, I can heal myself... do you feel any disturbance in your body?

C: I feel some tension in my back and legs.

[The therapist changes to tactile bilateral movements on her hands because the client has her eyes closed.]

C: The tension in my legs is gone. But I still feel some on my back (BLS). OK, it's gone. I'm light... see you at the next session!

T: You have three kinds of resources: internal, external and spiritual. Remember to use them.

C: The doctor who gave me the treatment told me to come back in six months for a re-evaluation. It's funny because I had tried to do the visualization before and had been unable to do so. Now it's like the field is clear.

The following day, when the client came in for a quick evaluation, she said:

C: I wasn't able to sleep at night. The little girl kept running around. I was greatly relieved. I remembered to take my medicine yesterday and today. I'm feeling confident. I think I've found my way. Now I need to persevere.

T: Now when you look at this picture [drawing #1 from the day before that the therapist had pulled out of her file] how much does it bother you now?

C: Two, because I still have this thing inside of me [tumor], but it's on its way out. Now I feel supported, whole. I'm supporting myself. I can see my alternatives, my choices, and do something about it. Before, it was someone else who had to do something about it. Now I decide who does what. I can deal with it. I have my new attitudes and new ways of dealing with things. I created this thing and I can "uncreate" it. When you said something about the medicine, something activated inside.

T: Your Internal Doctor?

C: Yes. Before, I used to think, I'm helpless and alone. That changed. Now I think, I can heal myself. I can get well.

T: On a scale of one to seven, how true do you feel those words are now?

C: Seven. I can be free, healthy and happy.

Some weeks later after this EMDR session, Rachel wrote me a note:

"I need to tell you how things have unfolded. Since the reprocessing continues after the session, on the following Tuesday I woke up with this thought: "I am going to find out exactly what is happening to me. And if there is any alteration in the tumor, I'm going to operate". I'm saying this, because I've been looking at my exams crosswise, you know what I mean?

"At the same time, I asked my husband (who was also against the surgery, out of sheer panic) to help me research what it is that I have. He's a doctor, but he deals poorly with family illnesses. That evening we talked it over, and he said that he had been reading up on it, and came to the conclusion that it might be better if I operated. He didn't even think it was necessary to talk to other colleagues.

"It was an enormous relief for me, and I told him I felt sure about my decision to operate, and get it over and done with quickly. I made an appointment with a surgeon for last Friday. And after that, I had this growing assuredness that it was good to get this things settled at once.

"Meanwhile, I started reading *Love, Medicine and Miracles*[29] (wonderful!) and that's when I really felt that surgery was one of my options for health. It is a choice within my reach. Why not use it?

"I was ready to go to the appointment with the surgeon on the insurance plan when I got a phone call, cancelling everything because he had had a complication with an operation. I re-scheduled it for a few days later, but on Sunday, a friend of mine who works in a well-known hospital asked me if I didn't want to consult with someone from there. She introduced me to a specialist who was considered one of the best in the country! So I had the chance to undergo surgery with her. I made the appointment for next week. I've got all of the pre-op exams scheduled as well, and I went to the heart specialist today.

"I continue to take my 'medicine': my visualizations of the piranhas, three times a day. Now I am able to do them. I'm also doing my daily meditations again.

"Everything is falling into place. I'm really decided, ready to do the surgery, recover quickly and go back to my professional life that I love!

"And I want to take the opportunity to thank you for all of your encouragement and support, and for helping me gear up for all of this."

"P.S. My little girl said to tell you that, "She's not going to tell anything to the other kids. She's just going to stick out her tongue and makes faces at them! LOL"

---

[29] Siegel, Bernie S. (2011) *Love, Medicine and Miracles*. William Morrow Paperbacks

A few weeks later, I got another e-mail from Rachel. She had just had surgery, with the doctor on the insurance plan, and everything had gone well. She was in the hospital for a few days, as people usually are after an operation like this. She was happy as a lark when they sent her home. That's when she really realized how opportune it had been to have it done:

"I'm home already, safe and sound! I don't have any complaints. Really I'm just grateful, especially after I found out from the lab report yesterday that the core of the tumor was beginning to go malignant. But what they took out had clean edges as well as the glands. So… I'm cured!

"Nothing is by accident, right, Esly? I keep going over this whole situation. It's amazing to see how important this whole journey has been, since the tumor was discovered. I see how many positive changes this illness has brought into my life. It has taken me places I would never have gone on my own. It was a course correction, a recovery of values in my life that had been dormant; a movement of understanding and deepening that I needed. It's had a very important role in my life, but now that it has fulfilled its function, like our dear friend Gilberto Gil says, 'out of here!'

"In my search for answers, I found new challenges, discoveries, and a new understanding. One of them was EMDR therapy, that gave me the strong basis to understand the causes of my illness, its meaning, tools to face it, and to reconnect with myself; and getting to know wonderful people in my life that are present in my life, some of whom are really special people.

"I can only be grateful, grateful, grateful and remember that I am here, not only for the difficult moments, but also to celebrate (a lot) my life as well.

"I especially wanted to thank you for indicating the book about *Love, Medicine and Miracles*. It was a fundamental piece in my healing process. That EMDR session was also important because after that I really wanted to get well, and sought out how to do that. And I found it!"

Epilogue

A few months after I began writing this book I was diagnosed with thyroid cancer. In fact, that is why this book took so long to come out.

It changed my life.

When I was 15 years old, the doctors found a nodule in my thyroid and put me under observation. I had gone to the doctor's office, innocently enough, to have my ears pierced. It was to have been my birthday present. My father would only let us do this with a doctor and it had been a battle to let his daughters get their ears pierced! Six months later, I knew the nodule had grown, so I alerted my parents and re-did the exams. Back then there was no such thing as a needle biopsy or ultrasound of any kind. The only way to find out whether or not the nodule was malignant was to operate.

This time I went to the doctor with my father. For the first time, the surgeon pronounced the dreaded word "*tumor*". I can still remember the cold chill that went up and down my spine when I heard him say it, and thought, "*Wow, I'm only 15 years old and I'm going to die.*" Back then, a cancer diagnosis was a death sentence, and tumors… were cancer.

Luckily, the nodule was benign. They took it out, left me the rest of my thyroid, and put me on medication for the rest of my life to supplement the decreased thyroid hormone production. That was the way it was done back then.

So many years later, the "souvenir" came back malignant. I could not believe that my body had betrayed me like that. This was something that happened to others, my colleagues, friends, patients, but not to me!

The weeks that followed were a fog of exams, medical appointments, decisions, until it came time to start facing the fact that I was going to have to go through this surgery all over again. Nobody deserves to have to go through thyroid surgery *twice*.

That's when I broke down. I called a friend and colleague in whom I trusted and asked her to help me with a couple of sessions of EMDR therapy. I realized that all of my childhood ghosts had come to visit. And it was a whole *gallery* of ghosts!

I had not realized that I had had so much physical pain, but during the first EMDR session it re-surfaced with a vengeance. I had not perceived that the imminent and constant threat of my parents' divorce had laid so heavy on me. I did not imagine that the silence about what a positive result during surgery could mean was so intense and that it could bother me so much even now, so many years later. It was two hours of sheer agony and relief. During the next session I was able to work on how I was going to face the second surgery, now as an adult. I knew I would be able to choose how I would go through the experience this time around: in a healthier manner, with less pain, both physical and emotional. And so it was.

Six months later, I feel like all I went through was just a surgical procedure, like the first time. I know that I went through radioactive treatment and that I will do check–ups for the rest of my life, like I've always done. I will take supplemental medication, like I always have, but now if I don't take it right I will go into serious hypothyroidism in a matter of days. The doctor says that he won't say I'm cured just because those ghastly five years haven't gone by, although he affirms my prognosis is fabulous… but sometimes remember I had a cancer diagnosis.

Many things have begun to change in my life. They are slow changes, but grounded. I want to spend more time with my daughter, and grandchildren. (My son-in-law is a pretty cool dude as well.) I had a tub installed in the bathroom close to my home office so that the grandchildren can better enjoy Grammie's house. I insist on bathing the new baby (in the kitchen sink for now!) And I throw a hissy fit if they don't show up at my house often enough, smile…

My husband and I are planning a special trip to celebrate our silver wedding anniversary. This is one trip I want to go on. But other trips I have passed off to colleagues. I want to write. I want to write *a lot*! Much more than I have written thus far. I'm in a hurry to do it. I really *want* to do it, to write down what I know. I'm in a hurry, but not pressured.

I'm changing roles. I no longer want to be the "Gets-It-Done" person, but rather, a supervisor, mentor, multiplier. I feel like I am a uterus, a womb: pregnant with so many projects, assured that God will give me life and health to bring it all to fruition.

When I began preparing to write this book, I stumbled across the ACE scale. I finally did the test and scored it. All of a sudden, so many things made sense. I understood what had happened to me. I began to understand what was happening to me now. I realized that it wasn't just the fact that I had had a complicated childhood. It had left me with greater consequences than I had imagined. There was a lot of stuff in my childhood that I had not been able to metabolize, even with so much psychotherapy. (Back then there wasn't any EMDR therapy, sniff...)

In ultimate analysis, while I was trying to explain to others about the traumatic childhood origin of disease that shows up in adult life, I wound up discovering… answers for myself. I am grateful that EMDR therapy allowed me to treat my pain, and that it opened doors to new possibilities. This book is the sterling result of it.

Author Biographical Notes

For more than 30 years **Esly Regina de Carvalho, Ph.D.**, has dedicated herself to the area of emotional health: as a psychologist in clinical practice; as a trainer in different modalities such as Psychodrama, EMDR and Crisis Intervention; as an author, sharing her experience with others. As an international presenter in three languages, she has taught and trained throughout Latin America, the United States, Portugal and Spain.

Esly first connected with EMDR (*Eye Movement Desensitization and Reprocessing*) in the United States in 1995, as a client while she was living in Colorado Springs. She walked away from that first session so impressed with the experience that she sought out specific training (1996/1997) in EMDR Therapy with the firm intention of eventually taking it to other Latin American countries, which she eventually did. When her husband was transferred to Ecuador, EMDR went with her.

By 2001, she had become an EMDR Institute Facilitator. While living in Dallas, she maintained a private practice in the city where she grew up as a child. In 2006, her husband was transferred once again, this time to her native country of Brazil, and that same year she was named Trainer of Trainers by the EMDR Institute. EMDR Iberoamérica was founded in 2007, and Esly Carvalho, Ph.D. was elected as president for the first two terms (2007-2010; 2010-2013). She is part of the training team in Latin America that trains professionals in Spanish and Portuguese.

Esly was certified as a Trainer, Educator, Practitioner (TEP) of Psychodrama by the *American Board of Examiners in Psychodrama, Sociometry and Group Psychotherapy* and passed her exams with distinction. She began training professionals in Ecuador in 1990, which eventually culminated in the establishment of a strong and vibrant Psychodrama movement in that country.

An international speaker in great demand, Esly has also published books and articles about the use of EMDR and Psychodrama. For those interested in her work, Esly has DVDs and books available in English or with English subtitles. Check out www.plazacounselingservices.com. She can be reached by e-mail (esly@plazacounselingservices.com) for those interested in her presentations in English, Spanish or Portuguese.

After having spent many years abroad, Esly presently resides in Brasilia, Brazil, where she is the Clinical Director of the TraumaClinic do Brasil, (www.traumaclinic.com.br), specialized in the treatment of trauma, anxiety and depression with the use of EMDR therapy. She is also president of TraumaClinic Edições, a small independent publishing house that offers titles on trauma, dissociation, reprocessing therapies and clinical strategies. She is dedicated to raising up a generation of professionals that are committed to helping people overcome the challenges of life.

Esly is happily married and dotes on her grandchildren who live nearby.

About the Author

Helping people overcome the challenges of life.

That's what I've been doing for over 30 years now. Although the love affair with psychotherapy probably started much earlier, I distinctly remember the first time I put a foot on a Psychodrama stage and thought to myself, "Self. You were born to do this thing". And you know what? I was. So I got trained to do it. Eventually, I trained others to do it. It was such a great way to teach. People really got it. They walked away with skills.

I grew up in two different countries, two different cultures and two different languages. Sometimes it got really difficult, but the balance was positive: I learned them both so well I became a native speaker of both English and Portuguese. As if that wasn't enough of a challenge, I moved to Ecuador with a young daughter and learned Spanish!

While I was there, I got married to this wonderful Canadian guy who got moved around a lot. I went along because he was worth it. As a result, I got more training in how to overcome the challenges of life. Some of it was up front and center. I was the one learning it for my own life. But some of challenge-training was professional. It came in the form of opportunities to learn by doing, in jobs, consultancy, courses and volunteer work.

And then I started writing. I had started writing so I wouldn't go insane during a nasty divorce from my first husband. I had to write or I would explode. That's when I wrote, *"When the Bond Breaks[30]"*. I found a voice I didn't know I had. Some of it was hard work, but I learned to enjoy it. I didn't always know where it was coming from, but I knew it was sacred. I just had to keep doing it. I couldn't stop.

With time, writing turned into articles. The articles turned into books. I never thought I could write long enough to get a whole book done. But I did. And then other books poured out. It was funny how some came out in one language and others in another. So I translated them. And then folks wanted them in the third language, so I got that done, too.

So now you know how it all happened.

What do I write about? I write about how we can overcome the challenges of life. Some of it is professional, but most of it is written for the

---

[30] http://amzn.to/1DweQWd - Available on Amazon.com in print and kindle.

gal/guy next door, so they can figure out what to do with their life, where to go for help, and what kind of help is out there. Sometimes I will tell you - but not too often - what I went through. What I'm going through. That's when I bleed a little. Most of the time, I tell other people's stories. Those are sacred, too, *especially* sacred, because we walked through the valley of the shadow of death together and came out on the other side.

You want to know how to overcome the challenges of life? Read some of my books. You just might find something there for you. Wanna know more? Come over to my website and pay me a visit www.plazacounselingservices.com. You can also "Like" me on Facebook https://www.facebook.com/eslycarvalhophd

If you liked this book, a review would be greatly appreciated. You can be part of the team that helps folks overcome the challenges of life, by getting the word out. http://amzn.to/1OZMaFm

Bruce County Public Library
1243 Mackenzie Rd.
Port Elgin ON N0H 2C6

Made in the USA
Middletown, DE
12 March 2016